Three Nights
in the
Heart of the Earth

Three Nights in the Heart of the Earth

A NOVEL

Brett Laidlaw

W·W· NORTON & COMPANY

NEW YORK · LONDON

The author is grateful to the Olin Fellowship, Department of English, Wesleyan University for support given to this project; and to Alfred A. Knopf, Inc., for permission to quote from "Of Modern Poetry" by Wallace Stevens, from *The Collected Poems of Wallace Stevens*, copyright 1942 by Wallace Stevens, renewed 1970 by Holly Stevens.

FIRST EDITION

The text of this book is composed in Caledonia, with display type set in Typositor Caslon. Composition and manufacturing by the Maple-Vail Book Manufacturing Group. Book design by Marjorie J. Flock.

Library of Congress Cataloging in Publication Data
Laidlaw, Brett.
  Three nights in the heart of the earth.

  I. Title.
PS3562.A332T48   1988   813'.54   87–24801

ISBN 0-393-02510-1

W. W. Norton & Company, Inc., 500 Fifth Avenue, New York, N.Y. 10110
W. W. Norton & Company Ltd., 37 Great Russell Street, London WC1B 3NU

1 2 3 4 5 6 7 8 9 0

FOR PAUL

Three Nights
in the
Heart of the Earth

As Jonah was three days and three nights in the belly of the whale, so shall the Son of Man be three days and three nights in the heart of the earth.

—MATTHEW 12:40

A day and a night

ULYSSES TURNER FRASER, my father, came from
the dark bedroom into the morning light of the upstairs landing. The tall windows that lit the staircase were white in the
low sun. Ulysses went into the bathroom. He combed his thin-
ning hair and pruned his red beard. He clipped stray hairs
from the corners of his thin pursed mouth. He shaved the
stubble from his flat cheeks. A small crescent scar shone red
below his left eye. His eyes were green.

He reappeared on the landing and returned into the bedroom. He emerged in a few minutes dressed in khaki trousers
and a blue oxford cloth shirt, with a dark sportcoat slung over
his shoulder. As he turned down the stairs he called,

—Colin, Bryce, morning!

I am Bryce; Colin is my brother, four years my elder. We
faced each other from our bedroom doors at opposite ends of
the landing. We squinted into the light and raised a hand good
morning.

I saw from the white sun that the day was cold again. Colin
took the bathroom first. I went into my parents' bedroom.
Today was my mother's forty-fifth birthday. Her name was
Elizabeth Gustafson Fraser; she was called Bitsy. Ulysses Turner
Fraser was better known as U.T.

In the dark bedroom I sat on U.T.'s side of the bed. Bitsy said good morning. I wished her happy birthday, and she roused herself and kissed my cheek. She pushed her dark hair back from her face. She said she was sleeping in. I left her to sleep and went to take my turn in the bathroom.

On the landing I passed Colin. He went into our parents' bedroom to wish Bitsy happy birthday.

Downstairs, U.T. had coffee on, and he was looking over the morning newspaper. Colin and I came into the kitchen.

—Good morning, sweet ladies, U.T. said.

The kitchen was warm and bright. The overhead light lit yellow-papered walls. We gathered around the breakfast bar that jutted from the outside wall. We divided the paper and drank our coffee. Colin said,

—Today is mother's birthday.

U.T. looked up from the paper.

—Is it? What day is it? It is. Bitsy's birthday. She would be . . .

I looked at Colin and he at me. I said,

—Forty-five.

—Forty-five. Be kind to your mother today, my sons, she's forty-five. That must be why she wouldn't get up.

He went to the refrigerator and took out bacon and eggs.

—In honor of this *journée fortunée,* this festive and significant annual recurrence, I shall make breakfast.

Then, as he flipped the bacon in the pan and cracked eggs into the grease, U.T. said,

—Birthdays: the ineluctable mementos of mortality.

Colin and I drank our coffee and read the paper. The radio on a side counter ran the morning news softly. It was the twenty-eighth of January, in the year of our Lord nineteen hundred and seventy-six. It was a futile time for birthdays, the dead gray heart of winter, when no birds sing, and when, in Minnesota, the snow has become crusty and gray, and the thought of spring is desperate.

I asked Colin about wrapping the presents, one from me and one from him, and a third from U.T., which Colin and I also had bought and would be obliged to wrap and address. U.T. turned from the stove and repeatedly pointed his finger at us, as if he had suddenly remembered something. He said,

—The tennis racket. You got it? Real gut?

I said we had, real gut. U.T. turned back to the stove. Colin and I agreed to wrap the presents after school. He was a senior at the University, and I was in my last year of high school. U.T. taught literature at the University and wrote poetry, besides.

I watched U.T. cooking. He was tall, over six feet, and he had to stoop slightly to tend to his eggs on the stove. His elbows stuck out as he handled the spatula, scooping fat over the eggs. There was a thin spot—not quite bald—on the back of his head of reddish hair.

In a few minutes U.T. placed breakfast before us. We ate, with thanks, and U.T. returned to the newspaper.

—The temperature hasn't been above freezing for fifty-five days, he said. One more day for a new record.

Colin responded through a mouthful of egg:

—Fifty-five, fifty-six, who cares?

—Such seemingly trivial data may signal a climatic imbalance of grave import, or presage the apocalypse, though I doubt it.

—I'll cross that bridge when I come to it, Colin said.

—Bridges have a way of sneaking up on you. Life is not an undulant path through pastoral glades. It's more like a turnpike, or the Boston expressway. You get in the wrong lane, and it's curtains.

We continued with breakfast, nonetheless. We finished our

second cups of coffee and Colin smoked a cigarette. I watched him attempt a smoke ring and noticed that his face was getting a little fat. His brown eyes were couched in sleepy pouches. It was a habit of mine to look for family resemblances; Colin seemed his own creation. I knew that my thin nose came from Bitsy, and my high cheekbones; my green eyes and knobbed chin were U.T.'s. Colin had a touch of U.T. around the mouth, the perpetual purse of the lips. That was all I could recognize. I considered that his thought had shaped his face, that Colin, who aspired to be a novelist, had willed his face to a blank, plastic mask, the better to accommodate the unknown lives of fiction. I considered, also, that his face was simply getting a little fat, as commonly happened to Minnesotans in winter. A permanent knit between Colin's eyebrows gave his face some relief. Dark stubble covered his round cheeks. Below the corners of his mouth there were white spots of skin where his beard did not grow. His mouth was set in a tired frown.

But Colin did quite well, this morning, to contain his discontent. He disliked being a professor's son, and he was not much good in the morning, as a rule. I thought he must have been touched by the birthday spirit. Or he was pleased with the weather, which confirmed his existential outlook. He was in the middle of his second novel, the saga of Marcos, a hero modeled on Colin's high school classmate of the same name. Marcos goes to South America and becomes a revolutionary. He experiments with drugs, sex and Marxism and gets killed for the privilege. Marcos, real or fictional, had held a place in Colin's heart and fiction since the two of them marched against Honeywell in 1972. I say the two of them, and of course there were more, but I had picked up an image from Colin—the unmoved duo pitted against the war machine. Sometimes I confused the two, though the novel was in the third person.

U.T. finished his coffee and clapped his hands. We bundled up for the cold. U.T. checked the thermometer outside the kitchen window.

—Eight below, he said.

We headed out the front door to the bus stop.

We lived on a lake, Lake of the Isles, in Minneapolis. Above the trees that rimmed the lakeside boulevard we could see the buildings of downtown, about a mile away. All along the curving boulevard there were large expensive houses, and small expensive houses, even decrepit expensive houses; you paid for the view. I liked to think that the eclectic architecture would spawn an avant-garde neighborhood, but my image of a progressive aristocracy was dashed daily at the bus stop, where we waited with the businessmen.

We took our place at the bus stop on a corner near the bridge that spanned the channel leading from Lake of the Isles to Cedar Lake. A chain of shallow lakes traversed the city's west side. Each lake was surrounded by expensive houses. The lakes were what remained of a glacial river that had run smack through Minneapolis, through the city's wealthiest neighborhoods. U.T. liked to initiate bus stop newcomers with this information. He would add that when the ice returned—as it surely would—the meltwater would come this way again. And there goes the neighborhood, literally. No one seemed to share U.T.'s glee in this image. U.T. waged a mostly silent war against the bus stop's stoic businessmen. He was the same age as most of them, and he was displeased with how his generation had turned out. He knew that it was not only his generation—he believed that Gertrude Stein's famous remark held true for all citizens of the twentieth century—but he could only take responsibility for one generation at a time. So U.T., the tallest person at the bus stop, would stand, biting his lip, looking over the businessmen's heads, trying to think of something to say that would snap them from their complacency. The enormity of the task left him silent.

This morning the businessmen stood in a tight circle and we shuffled coldly on the periphery. The businessmen wore long wool coats—gray, black, or camel—and neat lambswool or cashmere scarves tucked around the ties that pushed their jowly faces up on their heads. U.T. wore his dirty blue down parka and a blue and white Yale muffler wrapped twice around his throat. The businessmen wore seventy-dollar Florsheims sheathed in Totes. U.T. had on an ancient pair of deck shoes held together with cloth tape, a remnant of his prep school regalia. Colin wore a ratty sportcoat to promote the writer's image, and a loose black overcoat he had picked up at a yard sale. I looked like the average high school kid, as best I could tell, in my red ski jacket, jeans, and hiking boots. Neither Colin nor I had inherited U.T.'s height. We were shorter than most of the businessmen. I was a little taller than Colin, who was rather squat.

U.T. was well aware that the three of us were anomalous characters at this particular bus stop. He was alternately amused and annoyed. Generally, a truce was maintained, though sidewise glances were inevitable. U.T. averted his eyes from the *Wall Street Journals* tucked under each arm. He sometimes talked loudly to us to drown out words like "impacting" and "interface." Hear no evil, see no evil. This prevented him from speaking evil. He usually allowed himself the luxury of one or two well-considered comments when we were seated on the bus, out of earshot of the businessmen: "Have you noticed how they all have those big red veins on their noses?" or "How many do you suppose have the gout?"

As the bus pulled away from the lake on this morning, I

thought about Bitsy, asleep in the dark, in the warm bed. In a few minutes we were out of the trees and into the city. Cars were lined up on the edge of downtown, idling. Plumes of white exhaust slowly rose from each car and slowly spread like flared pillars; the city stood behind a white colonnade. Steam issued from smokestacks downtown; the steam hung and billowed like summer clouds. When it was this cold and this still the air seemed like glass, the buildings and sky painted on glass, as though it could all shatter and come tumbling down, the entire city in a jingling heap. I got off the bus at my school. U.T. and Colin continued on to the University.

❧

At ten o'clock I was involved with *Paradise Lost.* My English teacher, a wild-eyed woman with a crooked cheerless smile, spoke excitedly to the sullen, silent class.

—"Of man's first disobedience, and the fruit / Of that forbidden tree whose mortal taste / Brought death into the world, and all our woe, / With loss of Eden, till one greater Man / Restore us, and regain the blissful seat, / Sing!" Do you hear it? Listen to the music: "Sing, Heavenly Muse!"

She cocked her cold smile.

At ten o'clock I knew Bitsy was up. I imagined her waking to the empty house on her forty-fifth birthday.

I have imagined so much of this. Half of it is hearsay, another part lies, and all of it unassailably true. From what I felt and imagined I have made what I know; this is the only kind of knowledge, and the purest form of truth, if the question of truth seems pressing.

At ten o'clock I knew Bitsy was up. She woke to the sound of battered air. A helicopter was circling the neighborhood. As

Bitsy woke she knew there was a boy in trouble out in the snow. The helicopter was from the sheriff's patrol, searching for a runaway from the home for delinquent youth across the tracks that skirted the lake. The deep drumming echoed through the empty house. Bitsy put on her blue bathrobe and went downstairs. She put the coffee on to warm. Above, the helicopter hovered, knocking the day silly.

Bitsy looked out the kitchen window. She read the temperature, still below zero. She looked for a sign of the running boy. He would be cold, frightened, perhaps, or his sense was too hardened for fright. Either way, he was in trouble. Bitsy wondered what she would do if the young man on the lam came to the door.

The helicopter was gone; the air still rang. Bitsy picked up the scattered sections of newspaper on the counter. Colin had started the crossword puzzle. U.T. had left a note on the telephone memo pad: "Butter, bacon, burger, Bitsy, thanks. p.s.— happy b-day."

She took her coffee to the living room. It was a large room that ran the depth of the house. A red couch and three chairs were gathered around the fireplace. In the front tall windows looked out to the lake, and French doors gave out to the patio in the back. The dark mass of the baby grand, rarely played, guarded the patio entrance. Bitsy sat on the couch. She hugged her robe around her. Where was the running boy? She plotted her family's positions: Bryce at school, counting the days to graduation—commencement, as it was called; Ulysses lecturing to his ten o'clock modern poetry class, looking for some spark from the students of a new semester; Colin on some odyssey back and forth across the bridge that spanned the Mississippi and joined the two campuses of the University, East Bank, West Bank—nervous Colin who seemed so steady, looking for a place to rest.

She finished her coffee and realized she was forty-five. She was cold, the house was very cold. The morning was almost gone. She got up and stretched. She took her coffee cup to the kitchen. On the way upstairs she checked the thermostat; U.T. had set it down to sixty.

By half-past ten Bitsy was running around the lake wearing the jogging outfit U.T. had given her for her last birthday. U.T. only gave it to her. Colin and I bought it, wrapped it, and wrote the card: "Loving you always, Ulysses." One of those sappy store-bought cards with inane verse inside: "I love you when the sun does shine / And when the snow does snow. / Another year has come and gone / And I still love you so. . . ." To paraphrase. The card was our revenge on U.T., who took no interest in birthdays. He considered it presumptuous to claim a day and celebrate it as the day when one happened unconscious upon the world. What cause for joy here? But this year U.T. would give Bitsy a tennis racket strung with real gut, the Chris Evert model with a small grip. U.T. was not averse to suggesting gifts after Colin and I insisted that he must give them. We told him that Bitsy didn't like tennis, but he countered: she didn't like jogging, either, till he gave her the outfit. U.T.'s penchant for athletic gifts seemed strange even to us, but it had its logic: U.T. had Bitsy in training to be a survivor. He wanted her legs to be lean and strong, her back straight, her chin tight. He desired the certainty of firm quadriceps and sleek calves, signs of a confidence that would radiate both inward and out. He wanted her to enter rooms unnoticed and fill them quietly with her presence. He wanted to be sure that no one, not even acquaintances distant and forgotten, would ever imagine that she might be dead. He wanted her will to anneal as her muscles toned. More than anything, he wanted her to run a four-minute mile and become expert at the net.

As she ran around the lake Bitsy watched for icy spots on the path cleared of snow. She saw skaters moving more easily on the big oval rink. A skier kicked across the snowy lake like a long-legged water bug. Bitsy was the only runner to brave the cold, but she thought: a forty-fifth birthday is no time to slack off. This same pavement had passed beneath her feet so many times. She imagined that she was running around the seasons: through the slush of spring that sopped her socks; along the shimmering pavement in summer when the soles of her feet burned; through the fallen elm leaves in autumn, the crushed leaves roaring ahead of her; and now along the frozen lake at a slower pace as she dodged the slippery spots. If the lakeside path was the round of the earth, where was home?

She passed the tennis courts, the wire-mesh nets up to the metal net tape in snow. She counted the curves and coves to home and picked up her pace. When she came in sight of the patch of water kept open for ducks and geese, she was almost there. She sprinted around the final bend, sucking cold air that stung her throat. 'Cross the parkway, down the walk, up three steps and home.

Our house was two-story brick, turn-of-the-century. It had come as something of a gift from Bitsy's family, the Gustafsons of St. Paul via North Dakota. They had made a killing in soy bean futures early in the war, and moved to St. Paul a few years later. They owned an art gallery in Minneapolis where Bitsy worked as a clerk and exhibition designer. Bitsy and U.T. had come from the East when U.T. landed a job at the University. They had come prepared to rent something appropriate to an assistant professor's salary. Instead, they found a mortgage with their names on it, large down payment paid, reasonable monthly rates. A little pride was swallowed, and they moved in. The house was furnished. The swing of chance was stilled. They could never sell that house.

The house was not offensive in any way, but it took Bitsy and U.T. a while to feel at home there. Slowly they overcame the guilt that accompanied a smudge on the wall, a spill on the sofa, mud on the rug. They realized the evanescence of paint and upholstery and carpet. Still, they sometimes felt like guests in the home of wealthy friends.

When Bitsy came back from running she got a soda and sat by the dining room window. The blue curtains fell in long curves, framing the lake and boulevard in the small square panes. She sipped her soda and rubbed the ball of her bare right foot along the smooth wood floor. She looked out on the boulevard and watched the cars go by.

White winter sun slanted through the bare elms and dappled the coffee table behind which Bitsy sat. Her eye caught the curve of the drapery and followed it up to a cobweb on the ceiling. She checked the corners for more. Dark wainscoting ran around the room. Above it, the wall was papered in a small blue print. A long oak buffet reached down one wall. On top of the buffet were a silver coffee service and stacks of blue china plates. The dining room gave on to the kitchen behind, and to the foyer off the adjoining wall. In the kitchen the radio was on low. Bitsy picked up words of special emphasis. Someone, something was suspect. She rubbed her leg that was smooth and tight from running. She worked her fingers into the taut calf. Across the lake she saw the snow, the line of black trees, and the sharp blue sky, whitening toward the sun. It was like the Royal Wedgwood stacked on the buffet, the old family china.

Her eyes retreated from sky, trees, snow, and caught their own reflection in the window. She studied. Her hair was dark brown, shoulder length, with a few streaks of gray. Her face was still firm, save for a little pouching at the chin, and a few lines describing the corners of her eyes and the fall of her angled forehead. Her cheekbones were high, her eyebrows dark and full.

She had been Bitsy from earliest childhood—some grandparent had deemed Elizabeth much too big a name for such a little girl—and she had grown into it, in adolescence had been certifiably "cute"; and then had grown out of it. Her face had gained strength and shape with the years. I thought it was a fine face, distinctive and beautiful; she could no longer be called cute. So the name did not fit the face, but that is the nature of names which, as U.T. sometimes noted in moments of poetic despair, could not account for the infinite changes in every instant of a temporal object. Names existed for convenience, but they were often inconvenient or unfortunate.

Bitsy wiped away a drop of sweat that had settled in her eyebrow. The skier she had seen on the other side of the lake appeared from behind the large island halfway across the lake. Three geese circled in and skidded on to the water, scattering the ducks. Inside it was silent save for the radio's occasional stress. The skier's shadow repeated his swinging, kicking motions. The metal tips of his poles flashed as they sailed up behind him. Bitsy watched and imagined a da Vinci sketch of the skier's circular movements. She thought, "I am forty-five years old." Every birthday brought a similar declaration and a brief consideration of its meaning. She thought of forty-five years, not as a chunk of time, but as forty-five separate years, and forty-six birthdays, counting the first. Why birthdays, why years, why count at all? Maybe U.T. was right. Numbers, like names, carried expectations, but names and numbers were arbitrary signs. Their meaning was the meaning we gave them, and it was dangerous to think of them as fixed. The day was fluid, or solid, as we chose. The earth spun and circled and fled across space, or moved not at all in our small human terms.

The light on the lake slowly changed as the sun came over the trees and picked out crystals of snow. Bitsy saw her reflection alter as the shadows shifted on the glass. The shape of an elm branch fell across the right side of her face. The skier's motions blurred with distance, and the form of a swan on the lake flared white as it glided into the sun.

❧

While Bitsy sat by the window observing the qualities of light, I was in chemistry, ignoring specific gravities and thinking about birthdays. I remembered many, but only a few that I was sure were mine. The birthdays of my childhood all ran together in a swirl of balloons and streamers and ornamented cakes. I remembered going horseback riding for some birthday party; was it mine? No—my family had nothing to do with horses. Another image arose of a lump of small children scurrying through a lakeside amusement park like petitioners approaching the emperor. The children cower under the terrible lights. They cringe at the noise and frantic motions of the rides and the hawkers and the crowds. The years go hard. I recalled one birthday I knew was mine, because it was on film. The labeled canister held this memory fast: "Bryce's 8th birthday—Dinner and Croquet." Such was my family's idea of excitement. The dinner, at least, was memorable.

U.T. was filming. The camera jerked around the table, revealing each of the guests, squinting and smiling little-toothed smiles into the bright lights that Bitsy held up behind U.T. When the camera hit little Timmy from next door he ensured this party for posterity by throwing up into his baked beans. ("Too much excitement," was Bitsy's explanation whenever we watched the film.) The camera fled from Timmy's horrified visage and panned the astonished faces of the other children. They gawked beneath their gold and silver party hats. When the camera reached me I was smiling and hamming as if nothing had happened. To underscore my callous egotism, U.T. panned back for a close-up of Timmy, who was recovering from the shock and starting to sob over the mess on his plate. The frame dimmed and Bitsy ran into the picture to help Timmy. She wiped his chin with a napkin and lifted him from his seat. She looked into the camera; her face turned red and her mouth began moving furiously. Then her trembling hand filled the frame, and the scene ended with Bitsy leading Timmy out the door, turning back to have the last word with U.T.

There was only a little film left for the croquet match, which was called on account of darkness and insufficient equipment—two unbroken mallets and seven children.

Another, much more recent birthday came to mind. It was U.T.'s birthday in 1974. We were taking our August vacation on Lake Superior. We rented a boat out of Bayfield, Wisconsin, and sailed the Apostle Islands for a few days, visited the haunts of freshwater pirates, and highwaymen of the fur trade. It was beautiful there and the weather was fine. We cooked over driftwood fires on the island beaches, and sunned on deck or on the rocks that rose from several hundred feet of water that was too cold for swimming even in August.

We had a wonderful time for three or four days, then things turned miserable. U.T. became restless. He wanted to strike out for Duluth and up the North Shore. Bitsy said that was crazy. The lake was too big and our boat was too small. U.T. would not listen. He designated himself skipper, though Bitsy had done more sailing, having spent several summers with Hampton acquaintances during her years at Vassar. All U.T. remembered was that Bitsy came from North Dakota, where there was no water, at all. Bitsy remarked sarcastically on the lovely seacoast of Vermont. Colin and I sided with Bitsy, and the great North Shore expedition was shelved.

The same day, Colin began to brood; he missed his electric typewriter. U.T. chided him for having "lost touch with the physical word." U.T. always wrote longhand. Bitsy hid below deck, trying to contain her anger and salvage the vacation.

We did not sail at all that day. U.T. took the rubber dinghy and paddled to a rock, where he sat alone, reading. I braved the cold water and swam a short distance to another rock. Bitsy and Colin stayed on the boat. My nose burned and peeled.

The next day was U.T.'s birthday. I woke first and went on deck. Fog had come in, thick and cold, in the night. I could not see the island, less than fifty yards away. Bitsy came on deck behind me. She had a plan. It was U.T.'s birthday, and he was a captive birthday boy this year. She was determined to make him celebrate.

She enlisted my help, and we blew up balloons which she tied to the stays and mast. We blew for a long time; there must have been fifty of sixty balloons tied to the rigging. They bobbed damply in the gray air, looking not at all how balloons ought. They were a strange sight, and not altogether festive.

In a short while U.T. came on deck. He looked at the balloons, then at Bitsy and me. We smiled conspiratorially. Neither of us said a word. Bitsy kissed U.T., then went below to fix breakfast. U.T. silently considered the balloon-festooned rigging. He then took a penknife from his pocket and began slowly, almost dazedly, to pop the balloons. He popped them all and left the scraps dangling. Bitsy must have heard, but she stayed below until the last balloon was spent.

She came back on deck with breakfast and saw the balloon stubs, the colorful tatters strung along the rigging, like flags of defeated countries, or like popped balloons, things no longer partaking of Balloon. She said nothing. She looked at U.T., who was sitting cross-legged on top of the cabin, fiddling with a bit of rope. He looked at her calmly with his soft green eyes.

There was nothing to say. I thought none of us would ever speak again. Bitsy untied the scraps and threw them overboard. They floated, going nowhere.

Colin got up a while later and ended the silence by asking about the bright rubber scraps that surrounded the boat. No one answered him and he became angry and went below for the rest of the day.

My chemistry teacher held elements to a burner to show their various flames: sodium, orange; copper, green; lithium, white (a compound of lithium, actually, because, my teacher said, "Pure lithium will burn most furiously if exposed to the air; it's really a superb thing.").

I recalled one more birthday. Rather, I remembered how my actual birth had been misplaced in time through an erroneous memory of an old photograph. The story is this: I never knew my grandfather Fraser, for he died when I was very young. U.T. talked about him sparingly, but I counted the image of his face as my earliest memory. There was a photograph in the family album of Grandfather Fraser leaning against an old black Ford, a baby in each arm, each baby in a blanket. One baby was Colin, the other was me. I believed I remembered that moment. Grandfather Fraser was a small wiry man with a muscled neck and hollow cheeks. In the photograph he wore wire-rimmed glasses that glared in the sun. His hair was gray and wispy, swirling back over his high forehead. He wore a white shirt rolled up to the elbows and baggy wool trousers. He stood against the presumably green hills of Vermont, a baby in each arm, smiling a closed-mouthed smile into the camera. The car had an Indianhead hood ornament and chrome striping.

I had seen the photo once or twice when I was very young. The album had lain in the attic untouched for many years.

Then, one day when I was fifteen or so, I was looking through the album for a photo of old architecture for an art class I was taking, and I came across the photo of Grandfather Fraser, the car, the hills, and the two babies. But something was wrong: there was only one child in the picture. What had happened to Colin? Both stringy arms were cradled around the one child. I went down from the attic to ask Bitsy about it; I thought I had the wrong photograph. Bitsy said I did not. The baby in the photograph was Colin. Grandfather Fraser had died before I was born. It made sense, of course. Colin was four when I was born; Grandfather Fraser could not have held both of us in his arms, anyway. I had never bothered to make sense of it before.

I took the photo back to the attic and replaced it in the album. It was not particularly disturbing, but it threw things off a bit. The outline of history was off kilter. A hole had appeared in the holy descent of Bryce Gustafson Fraser. It was not that important, but I felt that I had somehow been tricked. I began to cultivate a distrust of memory, which is what this is all about. So: there.

At a quarter to eleven U.T. was standing at the podium in a deep, high-ceilinged auditorium, shouting at his class about "The Waste Land." He had gone through a half dozen cigarettes in the course of his lecture, and he kicked through the butts as he paced the stage. Fifteen students were clustered in the front rows of seats, some taking notes, some dozing, some looking to challenge, pushing their pens into uptilted chins. U.T. paused to think and took a long drag on his cigarette. He tugged at his bearded chin. He hunched over the podium. He said,

—"You know only a pile of broken images. . . ."

He extended a long arm toward the class and gestured vaguely with his fingers.

—Heap, sir, a chin-tilted student said.

—Very good. What?

—*Heap* of broken images, the word is *heap.*

U.T. dropped his cigarette and ground it out.

—Fine, "heap." "Son of Man, you cannot say or guess . . ." Well?

The class was speechless. The bell answered by ringing.

—Tomorrow, children, U.T. said. We'll consider the significance of the heap.

He took out another cigarette to entertain questions as he stepped from the stage. A student, a long-haired young woman named Caroline, lit his cigarette. She had been in U.T.'s classes before, and had made a habit of lighting U.T.'s post-lecture cigarette.

—Caroline, what do you know?

U.T. was wary of Caroline. Caroline said,

—How does this relate to Joyce?

U.T. tapped the ash from his cigarette and looked at the ceiling.

—Joyce, Joyce, Joyce. It doesn't but it does, in a sense, in terms of the response to chaos. There are various reactions to the sense of disintegration which we see in the writers of this era. Some were repulsed by the compulsion towards order and the realization of its artificiality. Some took up the task joyfully. All of them, by the simple virtue of their writing, had some part in putting things together again.

—The Humpty-Dumpty school of literary criticism, said a voice from the clump of students gathered behind Caroline.

—Call it what you will, but that's what literature is: Humpty-Dumpty Agonistes. Anybody can do it, or something like it, or it wouldn't be worth anything. It's all literature, really—living, thinking, seeing. The weight of the subject in the notion of the object, Cortázar called it. We all do it. That's what makes it fun.

Caroline cocked her head and spied a puzzled eye at U.T. He looked back at her, took a puff. He had dazzled his students again. They had been under the impression that literature was serious. They stood silent, waiting for an answer, or a cogent question. U.T. checked his watch.

—Gotta run, he said.

The students turned away and dispersed. As U.T. left the room he wondered where all that tuition was going, and how he could accept money for this. In the hallway he heard the boiler banging. The doorway was filled with a cloud of human exhaust from students pouring in for the next hour's class. As U.T. entered the brittle day he looked toward the river and saw streamers of mist rising and flowing around the bridge. He was on the East Bank looking west toward downtown. Tall buildings stood flat against the pale sky. Everywhere the air was rimed with the frozen exhaust of life and movement, but it was all very still. Cars flowed around a cloverleaf on the West Bank, students coursed across the bridge in two-way traffic that melted to stasis. Action and inaction had cross-multiplied and canceled each other out. U.T. stopped and watched.

A group of students passed by and brushed U.T. to the edge of the sidewalk. The world moved; U.T. blinked. He started on his way back to his office. A batch of papers awaited grading there. He thought ahead to the reading that night where he would be the featured poet. He had seen his black-and-white image on posters sprinkled around campus. It was only a small and cliquish band that attended the readings, but U.T. took his task seriously. This kind of weather was fine for poetry, a weather of extremes and high emotions. There would likely be a fire in the small room in the West Bank Union where the readings were staged. He could mix something warm with his own poems, some Frost, perhaps, or "The Wild Swans at Coole," or some softer Keats. He thought about digging out some of his own early efforts, poems about Vermont childhood, about cidering and sugaring, the thrilling and terrible grind of the seasons. Those lines had come easily, when his whole life was future and mistakes had no meaning, annulled as they were by eternity, in youth, on the uphill side of the long down spin to adulthood, resignation, when solid things suddenly refused to yield their meaning. U.T. took out his notebook and scribbled the first line of a poem: "I live in a world of adjectives, sprung and flung without nouns." In a couple of hours steady work he could have it ready for the reading. He switched paper grading to tomorrow and hurried down the snow-banked sidewalk.

❧

Bitsy had been sitting too long at the dining room windows. She had counted the panes in the three tall panels of windows—six across, eight high. She had called the gallery to say she wasn't feeling well and wouldn't be in today. She didn't like the people who worked at the gallery; her parents did all the hiring. She thought about the things one might do for oneself on one's birthday: shopping, a nice lunch and cocktails, a movie, a long bath. Action was called for. Her meditations were becoming morose. She fixed her thoughts on the boulevard, something that was going somewhere.

In summer, she liked to sit on the front steps on weekends and watch the cyclists whirring around the lake; she liked their muscled shaven calves, the grace and speed and the resignation in their down-turned eyes as they went around and around the lake. People came from all over to make circles around the lake. They loved the water.

Toward the water, as Bitsy watched, came a woman with a purpose. It was the old Latvian lady, walking with small fast steps down the boulevard. She came to feed the swans, her daily chore. The Latvian lady was short and round. She wore an old brown overcoat, and a red plaid scarf tied over her head and knotted at her chin. The skirt of a flowered dress showed below the hem of her overcoat.

Two clipped-winged trumpeters shifted about in the patch of open water, accompanied by a lone black male swan. The black was the Latvian lady's favorite; she called it Swanee. Bitsy heard her calling, heard her rattling her bag of crust and seed. The ducks and geese clustered around her feet and she waved her mittened hand to shoo them away, to clear an approach for the swans. They came to her, the trumpeters in front, Swanee, the black, behind. The Latvian lady seemed to curtsy as she bent to offer a hand of seed. She held the other birds off by tossing crusts to the side.

Bitsy thought this woman had chosen a worthy vocation. She thought she might like to talk to the Latvian lady, see if she would divulge the tricks of her trade. Bitsy could call to her and invite her in. She might see that the Latvian lady was not so old as she appeared in her loose ragged clothes. After a tour of the house, which the lady, perhaps, had admired these many years of swan-feeding, they would sit at the coffee table and share in tea and cakes. They would chat. Then, at the Latvian lady's request, Bitsy would take the bag of crust and seed and try her hand at calling the swans.

Maybe the Latvian lady would take to the lovely brick house and set up shop there, rallying her kin to join her. And when Bitsy returned the house would be filled with warmth as never before; filled also with what she would identify as the smells of

Latvian cooking, though if pressed, she couldn't honestly say where or what Latvia was. But it would all make sense. The Latvian men would make passes at her and pinch her athletic ass. They would be swarthy. They might have knocked out a few walls for a homier atmosphere. The halls would abound with livestock: goats would nibble the foyer rug; cocks and hens would scuttle through the kitchen; a fine young heifer would stand at ease in the living room, tethered to the baby grand. There would be Latvian babies, naked as God, crawling about, laughing, speaking new words at the world. The neighbors would be horrified.

But Bitsy would accept a plate and sit as a guest. She would let slip that today was her birthday, and such celebrating as she had never seen would break loose. The Latvian men would set her in the center of the living room and dance in a circle around her, clapping and leaping and shouting throaty Latvian cheers. They would take turns with her in the center, dancing with her and holding her in a manner much too familiar. They would dance till they were exhausted. They would end with special birthday toasts to ensure a long and fortunate life.

The mood would calm for folk tales, quiet singing, and the drinking of native cider. They would all reflect on their good fortune, and on some mysterious grace. The fire would fade, the livestock settle for the night. Then Bitsy would exchange good wishes, thank her hosts, and with her bag of crusts and seed go to test the ice and warm a place to sleep with the swans.

At lunchtime I rewrote an editorial endorsing Eugene McCarthy for president in the election more than nine months away. It was Colin's idea—early saturation. I was the editor of my school's newspaper. Colin had worked for McCarthy in '72;

U.T. and Bitsy had worked for McCarthy in '68, the big one. They had even traveled to New Hampshire for the primary. That had been U.T.'s last time in the East. I sometimes thought of Eugene McCarthy as a distant uncle, and with that I thought of Marcos as a brother or cousin. The ghost of Marcos haunted all things political or idealistic in our house. Colin's novel about Marcos was, I thought, a kind of mourning.

For where was Marcos? and who was he? His parents were foreigners and were rumored to be Communists, though they were known to be patrons of the arts. Marcos had left the country for Colombia before Nixon resigned and rumor had it that he was now a trained revolutionary. Colin's novel went from there, flashing back to the days when he and Marcos wrote libelous letters to various newspapers about various atrocities to which they had strongly objected. They had marched together all over the state. In order to do justice to Marcos's crusade, Colin had done extensive research on the flora and fauna, the cultural and political milieu of South America. The jungle, in particular, had gripped his imagination. He saw it as a great sprawling metaphor, something like Sandburg's Chicago, but more organic. It had spawned epithets worthy of Homer: the unanimous jungle, the woven-topped forest, primordial rain-garden, green-tented land. That was where Marcos now lived and approached his fate by the rules of the country, by the rules of imagination.

Actually, he approached the ending already written. Marcos is killed laying seige to a fortified village. He is shipped back to Minneapolis in a body bag, his remains unrecognizable. One small hunched man attends the funeral in a pauper's field and utters a prayer for Marcos. How the man knows this is Marcos beneath the unmarked grave is unclear. The man, we guess, is Colin.

A lone mourner stood by the grave of Marcos, the unmarked grave of the unknown hero. Rain settled the fresh-turned soil. The mourner knew, but could not justify giving a name to this.

The lines went down as Colin sat in a coffeehouse on the West Bank. Colin moved somewhat uneasily there amid the wreckage of the Sixties. He sipped coffee grown by independent Mexican farmers and thought about Marcos, thought that the Seventies had cheated them both. His mind was turning to art for art's sake, and the shops along Cedar Avenue, which where it intersected with Riverside formed the heart of the West Bank, were turning from left-wing bookstores and obscure cinemas to cooking shops and art supply stores.

Colin looked out on to Cedar–Riverside through the coffeehouse windows painted with slogans and announcements: Support the Cedar Court Rent Strike; Feminist Theatre, Saturday; March for Food, March for Human Rights, march for abortion and jobs and music and universal happiness. University students marched past the window. Ironically, the School of Business Administration had been placed on the West Bank. Colin saw briefcases and trenchcoats pass by attached to students who were barely post-pubescent. Cedar and Riverside were two streets that met in a dangerous intersection across which business students hurried. Cedar and Riverside also intersected somewhere in Colin's mind; that was where Marcos walked, Marcos of the wild eyes and the fierce beard, who could consume drugs, sex and Marxism, and die sated.

The story of Marcos was Colin's second novel. The first remained unfinished. It was the story of my sojourn east to prep school. I was not quite the novel's hero, but some kind of protagonistic metaphorical figure. It began: "Bryce is following the curve of a backward sun, arc-ing east on a line indirect and weightily tangential. He tracks a Fitzgerald dream of painless union and easeful discovery. Across the land he observes the machinations of humanity and geography and gleans some meaning from a drama old as dirt." I was, in fact, going to New Hampshire to boarding school, from which I returned after one semester. I was also going to the East of U.T., looking, I admit, for the second infant boy in the photograph of the man, the car, and the hills. But I found no mysteries, no resonance in the land. The hills were lovely, but hills cannot speak. The lawns of rural homesteads were dotted with plastic animals and windmills in pathetic pastoral scenes, and in the French sections with plaster Madonnas. That was a language I understood. Most places were pretty much the same except for topography, so I left, and returned home ashamed. To regain face I edited the newspaper, sang in the glee club, took photos for the yearbook, and played hockey.

Colin left the coffeehouse and turned toward the river, pointed himself at the East Bank for his eleven o'clock philosophy class. He thought about writing a letter to Marcos. Address it: Marcos, Revolutionary, South America. What was the zip code for South America? More than that, what could Colin say? Marcos would despise this kind of life, running to bells and classes and professors' demands. Wasn't that what Marcos had run from? No. Marcos had not run *from* anything; he had run *to* something. It was important to Colin that he know, for his novel, that thing worth going so far to find.

On the Washington Avenue Bridge Colin looked south. Ice covered the river and stretched south around a wide curve. Where it passed through Minneapolis the Mississippi was grand by reputation only. A strong arm could throw a stone across it, and it was cluttered with locks and dams and small islands, walled by decrepit mills and warehouses. Colin stopped and leaned against the railing and looked down at the gray ice streaked with snow. The bridge had two decks—a lower level of roadway supported a walkway above. Colin took a penny from his pocket and tossed it over the railing. It swirled and glinted as the wind carried it away from the bridge and down to the ice. Colin's legs shuddered as traffic passed below. His cheeks burned in the raw wind.

When he reached the East Bank Colin thought twice about philosophy. He decided to drop in on U.T. To get to the English department he walked across the Northrop Mall, a long court lined with buildings and bounded at the north end by Northrop Hall, a large auditorium above a wide set of stairs, whose colonnade façade faced the mall. The mall was a field of snow scarred with sidewalks. Colin crossed the mall and walked up the steps to the English department building. U.T. was in his office, at work on his new poem.

> I live in a world of adjectives
> Sprung and flung without nouns.
> Verbs, too, have fled, the life of things.
> I know by dim hints
> And I see the world softly and spread.
> The solid things silence; I cannot speak.

He had come up with "dim hints" after trying "cloudy clues," "cryptic cues," and "nebulous intimations." Colin knocked at the door.

—Enter, U.T. said.

Colin opened the door a crack and looked in. When he saw U.T. alone, he came in. He took off his overcoat and sat down. He took his cigarettes from his sportcoat pocket. The room was dirty and gray. The desk was covered with a mass of paper from which U.T. had carved an opening to work.

—I thought you were going to clean this place up, Colin said.

U.T. swept a look around the room.

—I did clean it up, but it didn't look professional. What class are you missing?

—Philosophy.

—Philosophy, a good class to miss. The mind founders in contemplation of the universal truth. I'm with Zeno, myself. I've tried to leave this room many times and found myself going forever only halfway.

—We're not reading Zeno. It's "Lights of the Enlightenment," or something like that.

—Why didn't you go to a good school? U.T. said. Why didn't you go to a real college? You're a smart kid, and your mother's rich. You could have gone anywhere.

Colin shrugged, looked away out the window.

U.T. reached for Colin's cigarettes. He examined the pack, took out a cigarette, lit it. Colin watched. U.T. looked at Colin.

—May I? I gave a half-pack lecture this morning, and I'm out, U.T. said, smoke trailing from his nose.

Colin waved his hand in consent. U.T. nodded and took another long pull.

—Filters, he said. If you're going to kill yourself you ought to at least do it with the real thing—Camels, or Luckies. We didn't know any better when I was a kid. We didn't know about lung cancer and heart disease and emphysema. I suppose if we had thought about it we might have guessed, but there were more important things to worry about—depressions and wars and related atrocities.

Colin smirked slightly.

—You don't have crises anymore like we had back then, U.T. said.

—I remember Viet Nam and Nixon.

—About as well as I remember the Great Depression.

—Better than that. I marched.

—It was all over but the shouting.

—I don't suppose it matters much.

—Not much. I'm bitterly disappointed with your generation.

—Sorry.

They both sat smoking. U.T. poured coffee from his mug into a styrofoam cup and handed it to Colin.

—Black coffee and cigarettes. No substitutions. How's the novel coming?

—Marcos is dead and his remains are on a plane to Minneapolis, or maybe the remains get lost in Houston. Anyway, he's dead.

—He never had a chance.

—No, you know from page one that Marcos dies. I don't think art needs suspense.

—Art, indeed. A good story is always nice. Keeps your readers busy while you perpetrate your art on them.

U.T. sipped his coffee. He fingered the page on which he had been writing. He picked it up and handed it across to Colin.

—Here's something new. See what you think.

Colin read the stanza. He exhaled a smoky sigh, coughed, and said,

—The rhythms are a little lame. And this grammatical imagery is pretty flat.

U.T. laughed.

—Thank you, Herr Professor Doktor Doktor. Your criticisms are always well-considered and immaculately phrased.

Colin shrugged.

—You asked.

U.T. nodded. Colin drank his coffee. He said,

—I had a very strange dream the other night. Want to hear it?

Now U.T. shrugged. Colin began:

—I was in some kind of store, a pet store, sort of. Bryce was with me, and there was a man I didn't know. He was the owner of the store. He was wearing a hat. He started bringing people out from the back of the store, as if Bryce and I were shopping for one of these people. It was like a fashion show. He'd wave his arm and these people would come into the store from the back. What was strange was that these people were dead. I didn't know most of them, any of them, really, but I knew, somehow, that they were dead. One of the people I knew: it was Grandma Fraser. She looked sad, sad to be dead, I'm sure. Her mouth was down-turned and her eyes were flat and blank. She looked right at me and didn't recognize me. I started crying. She went out where all the other dead people went out, and they kept coming. Bryce ran after her, then stopped. His arms dropped to his sides, and when he turned around I saw that he was crying, too.

Then the owner of the store changed. His face became a death's-head mask, and he became a character called "The Narrator," capital "N." Suddenly Bryce was gone and the Narrator was chasing me. He had horrible teeth and a red mouth, and a white, white face. He still wore the hat, a wide-brimmed black hat. He was chasing and taunting me, and I was running. Then, somehow, the Narrator became a puppet, on my hand, attached to my hand. I tried to tear it off, but I couldn't, and I kept running, though I couldn't run away from the Narrator since he was on my hand. I was scared shitless. The Narrator kept baring his teeth and jeering and laughing. I thought he was trying to hurt me, though he really couldn't. Finally, I was in some building, I think it was this one, and I ran into a stairwell; I fell down the stairs, and I tore the Narrator off my hand. He was on the floor, just a puppet, limp and still, and I stomped and pounded on him till I knew he was dead.

Colin paused. He sipped his coffee and continued.

—I was exhausted. I walked back up the stairs and opened the stairwell door. Someone was standing there, it might have been Bryce. I said, "The Narrator is dead." Then Bryce, or whoever it was, sort of grinned, and he pulled a hand from behind his back. On his hand was the Narrator, just like before, laughing and jeering with his flat dead eyes, like sharks' eyes. The person said, "The Narrator will never die!" I screamed, my heart seemed to stop, and then, as they say, I woke up.

Colin lit another cigarette.

—What do you think?

—You've got the wrong office. Go see Teasdale, our resident Freudian.

—What about this "Narrator" business, though? What do you think that means?

U.T. rubbed his eyes and pushed back in his chair.

—Maybe you fear that the assumption of the auctorial voice will destroy your own personality, you're edging toward schizophrenia, I don't know. I don't put much stock in dreams. Maybe it's just a good scary story. Put it in your novel, make it Marcos' dream. Change it from the Narrator to "The Revolutionary."

Colin brightened a little at the suggestion.

—Leave me now, U.T. said. I have to finish this piece regardless of what you think.

—I still think there's something to this dream.

—Maybe. Who knows where meaning lies?

Colin left. U.T. went back to his poem. He deleted the grammatical imagery and went on to the second stanza.

At a little after one o'clock Bitsy called the bakery and ordered a birthday cake. She got the kind U.T. liked, chocolate cake with white icing. She ate lunch alone and left the house to see an exhibit at the modern art museum on the edge of downtown. It was showing a special exhibition of Picasso's work, a traveling show that had stopped in the Midwest. Picasso was everywhere, on buses, on billboards, on limited edition wall-papers. Cosmetic counters in downtown department stores featured the colors of Picasso for your face to match your new wardrobe of Picasso-colored clothing.

Bitsy paid to park and walked to the museum. She entered the museum's wide lobby, where white walls rose thirty feet to a skylight. A crowd of people gathered around the ticket counter. Bitsy joined the crowd to buy her ticket, then followed the roped path that spiraled through the staggered galleries to the top floor. The crowd was thickest in the early works, around rosy acrobats and brooding self-portraits and things that looked real. She passed through surrealistic beach scenes, bulbous busts, found-object collage. At the end of the exhibition proper she came into "Homage to Piccaso," then "Picasso's Legacy."

She passed through "Picasso's Legacy" and walked up a long flight of stairs to the gallery that held the etchings, the Vollard Suite from Forth Worth. She looked at the studio scenes, where artists and models and art were confused in a melange of perspective and form. She saw Picasso's homage to Rembrandt: a bushy-bearded profusely etched Rembrandt taking a drink from the outline of a bartender. Bitsy tried to move with the flow of the crowd, which was going too fast for her. Only the etchings stood between the lookers and lunch in the restaurant one floor up.

She was coming to the end of the etchings when she stopped at an etching from the Minotaur series. She stood and studied, impeding traffic. In the etching a little girl with broad Hellenic features led the now blind Minotaur by the hand. She carried a candle; a dove had alighted on her shoulder. The girl and her candle shed light that reached almost to the corners of the print. The Minotaur, all furzy bullish head and wide shoulders, raised his head to the stars, his mouth, his thick dark lips, open in a cry. He carried a walking stick; his thick hips looked too stiff to move at all. The face of the girl was impassive, or perhaps there was even a slight smile on her thin lips. The light from the candle flowed over the black night behind the pair. The stars were like the last bits of mercury clinging to an old mirror.

The gallery blurb said that this etching reflected Picasso's fear of old age and impotence (artistic and otherwise), but expressed hope for the future through the girl, the dove, and the candle. Probably there were overtones of antiwar sentiments, as well. In other etchings the Minotaur was lying about in studios with naked artists and models, drinking wine. The fear of impotence was not apparent in these. Someone standing behind Bitsy made an art-gallery remark:

—Every line is so full with meaning.

A line came into Bitsy's head: *In the room the women come and go, talking of Michelangelo.* A touchstone line. *There will be time.* U.T. was always quoting those lines. But there wasn't time because the show closed today and the gallery was packed. She felt a shove. She wanted to look longer, weed out those overtones, but the crowd was hungry for new visions. The crowd moved her away from the etching, toward the stairs that led back down to the Blue Period.

She stepped out of the crowd at the far end of the long room. She leaned against a tall smoky window and looked down the cream-colored walls broken by frames. She turned and looked out through the darkened glass. She was looking east toward downtown, across the highway and a small park. The buildings rose in steps to a glass skyscraper in the center of the city. The Romanesque shape of St. Mark's cathedral was directly across the highway, and a few blocks north stood the Gothic Basilica of St. Mary. The two cathedrals framed her view of downtown.

Bitsy remembered coming to this museum shortly after we moved to Minneapolis. She and U.T. had wandered through on a Sunday afternoon when the galleries were nearly deserted. They talked about the paintings, and about the state of modern art. They were not optimistic. They did like Milton Avery, and Rothko. Bitsy liked the early Modernists—Picasso, Matisse, Cezanne, Bonnard. She wanted to continue liking modern art. She wanted to continue as a young woman with interests in the world, and not become a young wife. In Boston she had not worried about becoming a young wife. Now they had a house, an expensive house, settled jobs, children. U.T.'s hair was receding and getting redder. I was five and Colin was nine and U.T. was just beginning to realize that he was a father and would be a father for a very long time. He had just grown a beard. The beard was redder than his hair. They walked slowly through the galleries, then up the stairs to the restaurant.

They sat on the terrace drinking Medoc. It was a summer afternoon, going toward evening, and the sun had fallen behind a great mass of thunderclouds. U.T. remarked on the quality of the light, the sun's reflecting around and beneath the enormous bulk of cloud that was gray below and opalescent above. The strange refracted light bleached the walls of the basilica a stony white, setting it off from the green churchyard, dissolving its tall mass. Downtown, two cranes on top of buildings under construction formed facing crucifixes underlined by a department store sign.

U.T. said,

—This is the West, land of horizons and strange light.

Barely a stone's throw from the river, still, this was west. Bitsy had grown up in North Dakota. She had moved through this kind of light all her life. U.T., who was from Vermont, was amazed at the endless sprawl of prairie, which if it was not visible from the museum terrace, was nonetheless imminent.

They sipped red wine as the light faded and the air brightened with refracted light. The air took on subtle colors, and the museum closed.

Bitsy's memory slipped back further still, to college and to meeting U.T. They met at a mixer, or a poetry reading, or a football game. Bitsy couldn't remember where they had met first. U.T. invited her to the galleries at Yale. He mailed her photographs of paintings by Cezanne, Matisse, Renoir. Soon he was driving to Vassar in borrowed cars. Toward the end of his senior year he broke the Yale-to-Vassar speed record. His friends called the starting time from New Haven to Pough-keepsie and Bitsy's hallmates met him at the college gates with signs and pompoms while Bitsy waited in her room across the green. That was how she remembered it. She had made up the bit about the pompoms, though her memory tended more to the ironic than the sentimental. Maybe she was missing the point. She had derived the idea of pompoms from a false conception of earlier mind. But something had happened, some grand gesture. She marked time by U.T.'s gestures. They were signs of rebellion against the commonplace, against the years' slow stagnation. Lately they came less frequently, and with decreased fervor; the best of them were absurd and thoughtless. Bitsy thought that tonight, the poetry reading, would be occasion for a gesture. She speculated on the new phase; what would the next gesture bring?

A gesture: after breaking the Yale-to-Vassar speed record U.T. invited Bitsy to New York for the weekend. He rented a room at the Gramercy and took Bitsy to the few places he knew in Manhattan—the Algonquin, hoping to glimpse celebrity, the White Horse Tavern, to soak in the ambience of poetry's nether world. It was November. They wandered through the city, going nowhere. U.T. wore a large gray greatcoat with the collar turned up, trying to look like a photograph he had seen of the young Joyce in Paris. He had no beard then. His long face ended in a knobbed chin. Bitsy wore a fitted black coat and a black beret. Her short dark hair framed her pale face. She wore very red lipstick. U.T. pushed her up against the wrought-iron fence at the Museum of Natural History and kissed her, and told her that he loved her and wanted to marry her. Bitsy hugged him and her nose pressed against his throat. U.T. remarked that her nose was very cold. Bitsy wrote a postcard home, telling her parents she was on an art field trip.

They made love for the first time at the Gramercy. They felt the whole city around them. U.T. quoted her a line from Donne: "Busy old fool, unruly sun. . . . This bed thy center is, these walls, thy sphere." His poetic memory was endearing. Years later, when reminded of such moments, U.T. would say, "That's the problem with a literary relationship."

That night they lay together in rich surroundings, expensive rugs and draperies, dark paneled walls, in the dark, in the warm bed. They talked about where they would live when they were married. U.T. preferred the East and Bitsy had no desire to return home. U.T. had dreams of taking the Ivy League by storm, becoming a one-man establishment. For the moment they imagined a life something like the one they were living that night, rich and quiet. They imagined a house on Cape Cod: brisk autumn weekends with plump red goose-pimpled children running through the house; friends and colleagues and good wine; a devil-may-care attitude toward a life that was going always in the right direction, an automatic happiness machine.

They were married after Bitsy graduated. U.T. was in graduate school at Yale. Two years later they had a baby. Four years later they were living near Porter Square. U.T. was teaching in a small college outside of Boston and Bitsy was painting walls at a gallery in Cambridge. They had another baby. Two years later U.T. was teaching at another small college outside of Boston, and then another. There were a lot of small colleges outside of Boston, but U.T. began to fear that he would be junior faculty for the rest of his life or career. Bitsy had worked her way up through the staffs of several galleries between onsets of child-guilt, when she would quit her job to be with Colin and me. U.T. was often "between jobs," as well. Colin and I got a nicely rounded, if somewhat fragmented upbringing. We moved to Minneapolis in 1963. U.T. had finally found a tenure-track position. Eugene McCarthy and Hubert Humphrey were in the Senate. Humphrey would soon become vice-president.

Bitsy and U.T. gave up on Cape Cod for the time being, and settled for the tideless green waters of a city lake. As the years passed, the East faded from U.T.'s ambitions, but he continued to address himself to the East. He developed eastern idiosyncrasies that he had never had: he had cravings for egg creams and grinders; he invented an accent to replace the one he had lost at prep school and Yale. He devoted himself to the writings of expatriates and exiles. He was beginning to take account of his past, then he stopped, because the past was far away across the Mississippi and too confusing. He remembered the East and his life there as an object. He settled for an air of mystery and a colorful reputation. The past stood still as U.T. knew it could not. For Bitsy, the East was a few years elsewhere, and now she was home. Now she was ready to be home. U.T. could never understand this.

Bitsy turned away from the window and started back down through the galleries. The crowd was thinner now. She came through "Homage to Picasso" and into the gallery with Picasso's last works. In the entryway she stopped abruptly. The large open room was empty, except for one small woman standing alone in its center. Bitsy was disoriented, as if she had wandered into the wrong room at a party and disturbed an intimate moment of strangers. The woman stood strangely still, her head slightly cocked. Dark glasses covered her eyes. She wore a loose gray dress and white sneakers. She had dull brown hair mostly covered by a blue flowered kerchief. And she was blind. Bitsy had not seen the white cane that the woman held limply in her right hand, and when she saw it, she was even more confused. Her first instinct was to back away, to leave that room as quickly as she could. But she stayed, and looked.

The blind woman was not precisely in the center of the room. Precisely in the center of the large rectangular gallery was a sculpture, a large bronze sculpture of a shepherd cradling a lamb in his arms. The sculpture stood on a low platform. The shepherd was over seven feet tall. He had legs like pillars and a torso like a rough tree trunk. The lamb's head nodded against the shepherd's chest and its thin legs dangled across his abdomen. The shepherd had a cropped beard and short hair on his long head. He wore no clothes. The piece was great and rough, and beside it stood the blind woman, somewhat hunched. She began to move her head in slow diagonal motions. She scraped her cane in small circles on the floor. On the gallery walls hung large bright paintings, grotesque portraits. Fat drips of paint hung dry on the paintings.

Then Bitsy saw that the woman and the shepherd were not alone in the gallery. In the corner stood a gallery guard in blue pants, white shirt and black tie, and beside him was a young man with long brown hair and a dour expression. He wore dirty jeans and a T-shirt. The guard was looking at a small piece of paper. He nodded and gave the note back to the young man with the long hair. The young man turned and walked to where the blind woman stood. He took her hand without a word and led her to the foot of the statue. He eased her to her knees and placed her hands on the shepherd's feet. Her hands were white and chapped. The young man took her cane and stepped back. Bitsy still stood in the entryway, watching.

The woman rested for a moment with her hands on the large feet of the shepherd. Then she began to feel her way up the sculpture. She moved her hands along the calves thick as logs, over the thighs like enormous hams, across the hips, buttocks, and abdomen; she worked her fingers all along the great rough shape. She rose from her knees and moved in slow circles around the statue. In the man's arms she found the lamb, touched its head and eyes, and followed down its rippled back. Then she moved her palm up the man's arm, grasped the biceps and ascended the round of the shoulder, the curve of the neck. She slid both hands down the broad chest, and up again to the head. The gallery was quiet. The woman's fingers finally rested on the man's lips, the highest point she could reach, and lingered there. For a long moment her hands remained on the bronze lips as the woman stood on tiptoe, barely balanced. Bitsy's eyes were fixed on the lips, and the woman's hands.

The woman stood down and the gallery filled with sound. Bitsy turned and saw a group of school children coming up from the gallery below. The blind woman adjusted her scarf and reached for the young man. He took her hand and gave her back her cane and they moved along to the next gallery. As they left the young man dropped the note he had shown to the guard. Bitsy followed and picked it up. She read: "This woman has permission to touch the sculptures." It was initialed in an official hand. Bitsy stood for a moment looking at the note. She looked up and the blind woman and the young man were gone. She found them in the next gallery. She touched the young man's shoulder and handed him the note. He said nothing, did not nod or smile. Bitsy turned and walked quickly down through the rest of the galleries and out of the building.

Outside, the sun was very bright. Bitsy wiped a tear from her eye. She got in the car and drove to pick up her birthday cake.

❧

At one o'clock I was singing with the glee club. I had a solo in a gospel song called "If I Got My Ticket, Can I Ride?" My part went, "Hear a big talk of the judgment day (Lord, if I got my ticket, can I ride?), Ride away to Heaven this morning." I sang a fair second tenor and was a friend of the director. My solo was interrupted by late-comers stomping up the wooden risers that filled the room, a large room down a long hall, out of earshot of the classrooms. The room was cold; one wall was windows that let in a considerable draft.

We picked up the song again, and I sang my part well. U.T. had been helping me with it. He believed that all writers should be good singers. He never missed a chance to join in a barroom sing-along. I had reached the legal drinking age in August, and though the high school regulations prohibited me from drinking, they couldn't stop U.T. from taking me to bars. We sometimes went to Irish pubs in St. Paul, where college students and writers mixed with locals. U.T. and his friends would buy rounds, and some time during the evening U.T. always managed to gain the floor and sing "Some Enchanted Evening," *a capella*. McCafferty's was his favorite bar, where they always had live music. They served true pints of stout and everyone got into the spirit. The band took requests, mixed old favorites with IRA ballads. They always sang "Finnegan's Wake" for U.T. There was a dart board and an old Irish bartender whom everyone thought was great fun and a fine fellow, but who wasn't either of those things and was only thought to be so because that was how Irish bartenders ought to be. By closing time everything was as it ought to be. The patrons issued into the streets singing final refrains. They were glad to have been so moved by the songs of the oppressed, and were resolved to take action. They were glad to be with old friends and dedicated to staying in touch. They were inspired by human contact and thoughtless of the coming morning. They were drained and exalted. An evening at McCafferty's was like a wild Mass.

I put some of U.T.'s gusto into my part when it came around again. "He-hear a big ta-hawk of the ju-hudgment day-ay. . . ." The chorus came in grand and full behind me: "Lord, if I got my ticket, can I ride?" I waited through several spirited rounds of "Lord if I got—I got—my ticket—ticket, can I—can I—ride—ride?" This was one of several religious songs we were practicing for the spring concert. The grand finale would be the "Hallelujah Chorus," with the glee club, the women's choir, and the mixed choir all singing together. We weren't very good, but we were certainly loud, and with everybody standing and singing along quality would be secondary to volume and spirit. Still, the tenor section—which had lost three members to the baritones since the beginning of the year—was in trouble.

I listened for my cue and tried to remember the things U.T. had told me. It still seemed odd to me that U.T. had never raised objection—not even his usual good-natured bombast—to the religious songs we were singing. His break with the church and all religious rhetoric (*"Ride away—away to—heaven. . . ."*) had been angry and complete. He had been raised in a Calvinist home and had retained a doubtful faith. We attended (*"Lord, if I—Lord—I got my—Lord—I got my ticket. . . ."*) a Presbyterian church downtown. In the choice between Lutheran (Bitsy's faith) and Presbyterian, the latter won out because U.T. liked the idea of a secret elite and didn't like Luther's politics. Colin went through the instruction on being a good Presbyterian, learned not to worry about his lot in the predestination game, but when it came time *(". . . away to heaven—heaven—heaven—this. . . .")* for his confirmation it turned out that he had missed two classes and would not be allowed to join the church until the following year. Colin was only thirteen and badly shaken by this rebuke from the officers of God, and U.T. was furious and appalled. He had a long and angry talk with the pastor, who refused to discuss the matter on philosophical and moral grounds. Rules were rules, and you couldn't have a church without them. U.T. followed the meeting with a polemical letter to the church, cribbing from Thoreau. He said that the church would be a wonderful institution if only it got rid of its priests, and that they had "fallen behind the significance of their symbols." In order to illustrate this point and then be done with the symbols fully and finally, U.T. staged a mock confirmation ceremony, including a re-enactment of the virgin birth. Bitsy, however, refused to play the Virgin Mary. I had never seen her cry so hard. I started crying because Bitsy was crying. Colin, I am sure, had no idea what was going on, but he was probably glad to be confirmed after all. I only begin to understand as I think back. U.T. took no joy in the mockery. I believe now that he was serious and very bitter, and that he staged the event because he felt he had to. He had to mark this further disillusionment, another lost leg of belief. Another fiction had renounced itself when it might have made concessions to salvage a measure of faith and comfort. It died—this was what U.T. was saying—by the stupidity of history and an exaggerated sense of its own truth. The church took us off their mailing list. Colin and I sometimes went with Bitsy to St. Olaf's at Christmas or Easter.

I missed my entrance and we had to go back a few bars and do it again. I still wondered why U.T. put up with all this gospel shouting. Maybe it was for the sake of art. I got my cue this time and sang for the sake of art, High Holy Art.

❧

Colin found a place to rest in the East Bank Union. He took out his notebook and set down the Narrator dream, changing it into the third person. Then he picked up the Marcos story.

Marcos awoke and looked through the tilted door frame into the tropical glare of dawn. Women traversed the square carrying water. Small fires of twigs and grass put a smoky roof over the village. Marcos went out and joined a group of men by one of the fires. They stirred to salute but Marcos set them at ease with a wave of his hand. He sat and took a bowl of strong coffee and raw milk. He chewed a piece of bread, dipping it in his coffee. He called to a young soldier across the fire. "Ruiz, someone must go for Ramon." Ruiz leapt at the mention of Ramon. "I will go," he said, and taking a piece of bread for the journey, started off at a trot into the jungle.

Colin checked his watch; it was one-thirty. Marcos's breakfast made him hungry. He went downstairs in the Union and got a sandwich and a cup of coffee. He sat alone, watching the room for friendly faces. He was a peripheral member of a group of intellectual toughs who carried tattered volumes of Rimbaud in the pockets of their leather jackets and stood at bars drinking beer and talking about poetry. There was no one he knew in the room. The faces of the students kept getting younger.

Colin thought ahead to the reading. He imagined himself at the podium, reading from his novel. There was opportunity for him to read after the featured writers had finished and the stage was thrown open to all comers, but Colin never ventured to the stage. He had seen the kind of people who climbed to the podium uninvited. If they were not miserable they were surely naive, and foolish to present themselves among the miserable. Colin would wait to be asked. He was known through U.T., and that association saddled him with expectations. U.T. bore the burden of Eliot, and Colin the burden of U.T. In a choice between T.S. and U.T., Colin guessed he would pick the former.

As Colin ate he remembered how U.T. used to read to us. Not children's stories or nursery rhymes, but Dickens and Scott, then Byron, Shakespeare, Keats, Joyce and Yeats. U.T. wanted the great works and the great sense of the world to reach us subconsciously. He was trying to create a new breed of poetic man, to whom metaphor would be second nature (at least), for whom the world would be a poem, waiting to be scanned. Colin tried to remember when U.T. had stopped reading to us. He thought that there would be some significance in that moment, some subtle change of consciousness in us and in him. It may, of course, simply have been that we lost interest or became old enough to protest. But then Colin realized that U.T. had never stopped. He still quoted constantly from his favorite poems. Colin checked his memory and found that he could recite all or part of at least thirty poems. It was merely U.T.'s tactics that had changed; his goal was still the same.

It was warm in the Union and the room was filled with the buzz of conversation. Here and there students sat alone eating or reading, looking self-conscious. This was no place for loners. The school was more than large enough to get lost in, and many did, but the results could be dangerous. Colin knew the strange ideas that came from walking alone, the melancholy and looming significance, the sense that in one's solitude one is waiting and watching, for something, or that one has already missed it. Things were being said all around. Colin remembered his next class. He gathered up his books and pages and went at a fast walk up the stairs and out of the building.

The light in U.T.'s office seemed indirect, as if the bright dirty window radiated the light it gathered, instead of allowing it to pass. It was four o'clock and U.T. sat, sipping cold coffee, in a cloud of cigarette smoke, going through a sheaf of paper, his poems. Interspersed with the poems were notebook pages, ideas for new poems, new voice from the old language. U.T. switched on the desk lamp; the window faded to gray, and the hazy sun, descending on the low winter slant, slid behind the buildings on the West Bank. The notebook pages were headed with dates: 22 October, 1957; 14 May, 1962; 17 January, 1974. Arbitrary dates, insignificant figures. U.T. calculated in his head the possible correlations of the dates. The idea of order on the East Bank.

U.T. heard the snap of the lock on the English department door closing for the night. He heard good-byes from the secretaries and departing professors. He was hidden away, listening. The weak light of the desk lamp showed smudges and watermarks on the walls and on the drop-panel ceiling. Aside from the desk and chair, the room held an armchair in front of the desk and a small table between the desk and the radiator below the window. A large jade plant, its tumid dark green leaves shining even through the dust and cigarette ash, sat on the table. U.T. sat for a moment looking at the plant. Its trunk was thick and as rough as a tree. It rose distinct a foot or so, then was lost in a tangle of pale branches which curved and crisscrossed, making wave shapes, graceful artless arches. The shape of the plant was a swelling mass; each branch sent out new arms, each arm swelled new leaves, teardrop succulents, and at each juncture there grew air-locked roots, ready to reach for earth if a branch should fall from its delicate cleavage. U.T. reached across the desk and picked up a leaf that had fallen from the plant. He squeezed it gently and liquid swelled from its pores. He reached across the desk again and stuck the branch end of the leaf in the soil. It would grow there, regenerate, and then the leaf would sag and rot to clear the way for the new generation. Its liquid would seep from the pores and into the soil and its cells would collapse.

U.T. turned back to his pages. He pulled a notebook entry from between poems. It was dated 11 March, 1956; Boston. He read it over to see how the conditional truth of 1956 had held up over the past twenty years.

The hills of my home country were mere conceit, for I knew what was behind them, knew the vista of each turn of the trail or road. They created a swirling labyrinth to which I had the key, and so was no labyrinth at all; a maze amazes only the unknowing. I knew the holes and hollows in the hills that seemed solid. I could slip through the façade to the sacred inner space, find the secret heart of the sculpture and know the artist's dark purpose.

In my mind I held a map of the country all around. The names of the towns were like totems, concrete metaphors surviving from the first day of naming. Call this Monadnock, and this Hillsboro, here Chesterfield, Pownal, Putney, and Sexton's River. They might as well have been called Name of God, Devil's Eye, Christ-Wound, Death in the Morning, Cult of the Sparrow. The names were nothing and everything, perfect signifiers, each unique and graven for its meaning, the small distinctions making up a cosmos. Everything had its role in the drama of the hills, and I was a skilled exegete. [U.T.'s marginal note: Did I really believe this?]

The contradance. We drove to Concord for the big dance at the New Hampshire Historical Society. I stood on the circular balcony above the rotunda and below the great dome, and looked down as the women and men in fine dress promenaded down the polished marble floor. I stood in half-darkness and peered down into the fine light below. The granite walls glittered through the darkness around me. The lighted dome was a golden bowl. [Note: I was reading James!] I heard the excited clogging, but better still, I heard the soft flush of the ladies' wide skirts, the grace notes of the dance. I was 17 and overcome by nostalgia in advance of my departure for college the next fall. [Note: Yes.] I was already imagining my town as a rock, from which I would be but a shed splinter, waiting, from the day of my departure and before, only to cleave again and bestow the boon of knowledge on my people. Fond youthful dreams. I hungered already for the histories I was leaving behind. As children we had made gravestone rubbings in the town cemetery and hung them on our bedroom walls. They were all our kin, familiar names long dead but near to us and we knew ourselves as the posterity towards which they all had looked. One was born at a place, at a time, and one died somewhere else, another time, and that leap is finally nothing. It seemed like fate, or else how does one account? Contained within that span between the specific birth and the mortal interruption of anniversary was the one great chance, the whole known to the survivors. The afterlife was in memory, the solemn duty of *comitatus*. We held high the memory until we saw its tragic side, its fragility and fickleness. [Note: I got that right. Why is history so jealous and fleeting? There is no truth in history, for history will justify anything; it is cruelly amoral or perfectly just, as the present's light fails or brightens.]

The dance: in my mind it is now a stately minuet. That is memory. I hear a harpsichord in place of the mandolin, fiddle, accordion and banjo. I see evening clothes over flannel shirts, dungarees, and rough-sewn dresses. To the sound of the fiddle the couples danced their paces. This was nothing learned. The folk simply knew the steps, and their names: sashay, cast-off, dos-si-dos, swing-your-lady, promenade. Corner lady, corner gent; home again.

I brought Bitsy up one year for the New Year's dance. I walked her around town and she moved beside me without effort, her throat white in the light off the snow, her face white and beautiful in the tight cold; the only sign of tension in the whole of her existence was in her gloved hand that squeezed mine. It was bitter cold and the snow creaked under our feet. I pointed out the best sugar bush, the way through the hills to the falls, I named all the houses and described the children, my friends, who had grown up within. I showed her the great beech tree where the girls had made fairy circles and conducted long autumnal processions to offer colored leaves to the god of the big beech. I kissed her under the beech tree and she laughed. How odd it was to her, that I came from this rich place and seemed to bear no trace.

If this is a lesson, I do not know the moral, or the punchline, as it may be. O lost! I am the sad ghost of a bloodless coup. I am invisible, my substance sucked away by slow loss. When I returned I brought no boon, there was nothing I could give. At the dance that night I was awkward, falling behind and losing my place. I attributed it to lack of practice, but it was more than that, loss of instinct, loss of certainty that had always been unconscious, and the harder I thought about the next move, when to swing and when to circle, it slipped ever further away. Bitsy had a fine time, enjoyed my family and friends, but I saw from their courtesy that we were strangers, both of us.

U.T. finished reading and slipped the pages back into the sheaf of poems. He wondered at the ferocity of those young words, and at their sure sense of loss. He remembered the dances again, through yet another lens, another mind, and the image which arose was one of gilded figures twirling atop a music box, serene and implacable, walking their paces to silence, the mechanism of music long frozen. The black window reflected dustily the desk lamp's light. U.T.'s thoughts worked along the rhythm of silence. From out in the corridor the custodian's shuffle intruded into the silence. The radiator punctuated silence with its occasional dissonant voice. U.T. looked at the jade plant on its table by the radiator, and his eye caught a glint of pale green on a dark leaf. He looked again, and again saw movement, a translucent flutter in the pale light. He trained his eye to the spot on the leaf and made out an insect shape, a katydid he guessed, on the jade leaf. The katydid began to sing; scraping legs and wings in an urgent blur it filled the room with sound that seemed to issue from the walls. U.T. was suddenly weary. He tipped his chair back against the wall and propped his feet on the desk. The katydid sang on the jade plant, the song of a small miracle in the northern winter. U.T. gave no thought to cause. Instead, he thought about Chinese cricket cages. He remembered hearing that they were sometimes made from gourds grown inside jade molds that were carved with landscapes and cryptic characters. The gourd grew through the mold and was then cleaned and dried, an ornate globe to encompass the cricket and its song. Peasants kept the tiny intricate cages in their breast pockets, where the cricket sang against their hearts, kept them warm and happy and gave to them long life. The cricket enjoyed a revered incarceration, but its song was the thing, since a cricket did not live so long as the life it endowed. A continuous line of crickets filled the role of the caged singer, the same unwearying song. In the small office the katydid had a whole jade plant for its perch. U.T. imagined carrying the jade plant about on his head, the katydid above calling out his arrival; he would be absolved of the need to speak. In addition, it was said that a cricket's chirping, rightly computed, told the temperature, so U.T.'s companion would give joy and long life and the weather report, all at once. Who could object to anything so small and yet so useful?

As U.T. watched, the katydid folded its wings and settled into silence. The radiator shuddered again, and a rush of wind rattled the window, sending a draft across the desk that shifted the pile of papers. U.T. fingered his chin and rubbed the day's stubble on his throat. With his finger he traced the line of his beard, a red beard flecked with gray. He touched the small scar on his left cheek; he felt the loose dark skin beneath his eyes; he rubbed his eyes. He was tired, and the katydid continued its pause.

Tipping himself back to the desk, U.T. picked up the sheaf of poems and made his selection for the reading. He drew a wide range of seasonal poems, counting on the context of a packed house and a cozy fire. Drawing from the sheaf those poems that he remembered as superior, he was disappointed at their actuality on the page. It was too late to rewrite, though perhaps he could make some changes as he read. Somehow the expression always slanted toward imperfection over time. He envied the perfect and immediate voice of the katydid, the ability to sing and cease at will, to offer no explanations. With a twinge of fraudulence he gathered up the pages and slipped them into his bag.

There was a knock at the door. U.T. began to rise and the door opened. The custodian looked in.

—I saw the light, wondered if someone was still here.

U.T. checked his watch; dinner would be waiting, Bitsy's birthday dinner. He closed his bag.

—Just leaving, he said.

The custodian nodded and closed the door. U.T. walked to the door and stopped, his hand on the light switch, to look at the katydid, which sat still, still and silent, a lighter smudge on the mass of plant. That tangle of leaf and branch was a hard thing to sing, U.T. thought. Rest was in order. He switched off the light and walked out of the dark office and into the hallway.

Bitsy was cooking dinner when U.T. arrived home. Colin and I sat in the dining room, passing a box of crackers between us, because it was late and Bitsy had waited dinner for U.T. We heard him enter through the back door. He came into the kitchen followed by our cat, Molly Bloom.

—Good evening, Elizabeth, he said to Bitsy, who was busy at the stove.

He kissed her cheek, and saw the birthday cake on the counter.

—Happy birthday, as they say, he said.

He came into the dining room and dropped his bag in a corner. He slung his coat over a chair.

—My sons, hello, he said, making a motion as of doffing a cap.

—Hi Dad, I said.

Colin raised a cracker in salute. He said,

—Late again.

—Not so late. I was picking poems for the reading.

He headed back into the kitchen and sat on a stool at the breakfast bar. He ran a hand over his short hair. Molly Bloom jumped on to the bar and U.T. petted her. The cat was very old, losing her teeth, and trusted no one but U.T. Bitsy turned from the stove at the sound of the cat landing on the counter. This was not allowed. U.T. took Molly Bloom into his lap.

—Another hard day in dear dirty Dublin, Molly dear, he said

—How hard? Bitsy asked.

—Molly! Did you speak? 'Tis a miracle I behold!

—It was me, Bitsy said.

—Lord, you had me going.

—How hard was your day, and how was it hard?

Bitsy poked at a pan of fried potatoes.

—Their minds are turning to custard, Elizabeth. They haven't even the simple language sense of native speakers. They don't understand a thing I say. And that Caroline, you know the one, rather pretty, long brown hair, intense look on her face all the time; she's after something. I don't trust her.

Bitsy laughed.

—What could she want? Your first edition of the Cantos?

She shook her head in amusement as she flicked at the potatoes, her free hand on her hip.

—You may laugh, but our children are grown devious.

—Possibly, some, not mine.

—All of them. What they want mostly is money. They never make a move without plotting it. They're in cahoots with the University; the College of Liberal Arts is becoming a farm team for the M.B.A. machine.

—Caroline wants your money? Wrong tree.

—I get the feeling Caroline wants to be my disciple—do people still have disciples?—or my concubine. She's a modern poetry groupie.

—The poor girl probably just has a crush on you—older, bearded, balding, you smoke.

—Please, you'll swell my head.

Colin called into the kitchen through a mouthful of cracker:

—When's dinner?

—Soon as it's ready, U.T. answered. Who are you to make demands?

Colin got up and went upstairs. Left alone with my crackers, I went into the kitchen and took the stool next to U.T. He put his arm across my shoulders.

—Come here often? he said.

—I'm drinking to forget.

Molly Bloom looked up from U.T.'s lap and hissed at me, baring her few sound teeth, then edged out of the lap and sulked away. U.T. looked sadly after her.

—I don't think she remembers people from one day to the next. And she pissed on my shoes in the closet again.

—I think it's time to send her to the farm, I said.

U.T. scowled. His cheeks were still red from the cold. There were drops of moisture in his mustache where his frozen breath had melted. He stood up, ran a hand over his beard, and went upstairs to change for the reading.

I stayed in the kitchen with Bitsy. I told her about my day, how I had been thinking about birthdays. I said,

—Remember Dad's birthday on the boat, with the balloons?

She laughed. I was glad she laughed. Then I reminded her of my eighth birthday—the one on film—and poor Timmy from next door. She still did not think that was very funny. We talked for a few minutes, then Bitsy went to the oven, opened it, and poked a fork in the roast. She stood up, brushed a wave of hair back from her cheek, and announced in a tired voice,

—Dinner's ready.

I went to the bottom of the stairs and called Colin and U.T. I heard Colin's grumbled reply and went to the table.

Dinner was roast beef, fried potatoes, cauliflower browned in butter, and salad. It was U.T.'s favorite dinner, the dinner we seemed to have on all special occasions. Bitsy remarked on the cobweb which still clung to the ceiling. U.T. told us his line-up of poems. He added Stevens, "Of Modern Poetry," and Yeats, "The Wild Swans at Coole." Colin expressed his dislike of the latter, and U.T. said that he was free to absent himself at the appropriate time. Bitsy mentioned that she had seen the Picasso exhibit. The show was very good, she said, though the museum was too crowded. The exhibition closed today; all that would remain of Picasso would be the buses, the billboards and, of course, his legacy.

I told Colin that the editorial endorsing McCarthy would see print in a week, and he was pleased, though he conceded that McCarthy didn't stand a chance. After uttering the name of McCarthy, Colin took on a strange look; his chewing slowed and his eyes dimmed. His fork reached automatically for another bite.

—Eugene McCarthy, U.T. said. I remember the great days in New Hampshire, in '68.

—The big one, Bitsy said. He kissed me once. I didn't wash my face for a week. How stupid.

The table became quiet. I didn't know what to say while Bitsy, Colin and U.T. stared dumbly at their plates, so I said,

—Not that many kids in my school can even vote, Colin. And those who can are mostly Republicans, I think.

That was not the right thing to say, or maybe it didn't matter. At any rate, Colin didn't respond. U.T. was the first to come around.

—It's going down to thirty below tonight. We are in line

for a record low, plus a record for below zero days, in addition to the almost certain record for consecutive days below freezing. This is a great time to be alive, auspicious days, these.

—In other words, it's cold, Colin said.

—You'd make a damn fine editor.

Bitsy removed a piece of gristle on to her fork and looked out the window. While the thought of these great cold days settled, Bitsy imagined the blind woman building a snow man, fashioning a perfect being from winter's refuse.

Colin thought: *Marcos remembered the days and hard nights of brutal cold. In the glacial north. The burning, biting, killing cold. There could be no revolution in the land of frozen minds, no enlightenment for the people of ice, plodding along in their snowy tracks, following, snow blind, the stupid track of their ancestors into Puritan oblivion.*

U.T. said,

—*We are the hollow men, we are the stuffed men, leaning together, headpiece filled with straw.* That might be a good one. A little more accessible than Stevens, and the politicos might like it.

Bitsy got up to clear the table. As she returned with cake and a cardboard carton of ice cream, U.T. checked his watch.

—No time for cake, he said, we must be off. Grab your coat, Col.

Colin looked sadly at the cake. He went to the hallway and put on his coat. The presents lay in their clumsy wrapping, unopened, the cake uncut. U.T. leaned over and kissed Bitsy on the cheek. As he slipped into his parka and picked up his bag he said,

—Sorry to miss the party. Sure you won't come?

—Someone has to eat this cake, Bitsy said. We'll be with you in spirit. Dedicate one to me. Say, "This poem is dedicated to my lovely wife Elizabeth, who, bless her soul, cannot sit through poetry readings. She feels badly about this, but she is stuck at home with an entire birthday cake and a half gallon of ice cream which she feels morally obliged to consume single-handedly." That will win their undying sympathy.

—They'll think I've driven you to obesity. I'll just dedicate my best poem to you, and let them wonder. Bryce? You're invited too.

—Homework, I said. But you don't have to dedicate anything to me.

—I had no intention of doing so.

—Don't be mean, Bitsy said.

—I'm not mean. It's almost impossible to earn a dedication in less than, say, forty-five years.

—Then I made it just in time, Bitsy said.

—No, I lied. I've been dedicating poems to you since you were nineteen. But it was risky. I gambled that by the time you were forty-five you'd have earned all those dedications.

—And?

—And?

—Have I?

—As they say, if you don't know by now. . . .

Bitsy laughed. U.T. kissed her again, and said,

—We won't be late.

From the back hall Colin said,

—No later than closing time.

U.T. scowled. Then he nodded toward the pile of three presents on the buffet and said,

—Mine's a tennis racket, real gut.

One clearly was a tennis racket. U.T. waved and followed Colin out the back.

Bitsy and I sat quietly for a moment, waited for the sound of the car starting, and the muffled crackle of the tires in the icy alley. I handed Bitsy the knife to cut the cake, and then went to pour coffee. When I returned Bitsy was looking at the knife, the cake still uncut.

—Do the honors, Mother, I said. Let's have a party.

She smiled, and reached for the cake. I told her to make a wish before she cut; she nodded, and cut a large slice for me, a smaller one for herself. As we began to eat she said,

—Do you want to know what I wished?

—You can't tell, or it won't come true.

—Well, I'll tell you anyway, since it can't come true. I wished we had gone to the reading. It means a lot to your father, though he won't admit it. I guess it's stupid to waste a wish on something I could have had so easily.

I stopped with my fork halfway to my mouth, and I knew Bitsy was right, that we should have gone to the reading. I had been thinking badly of U.T. for leaving the birthday dinner, but Bitsy was right, and U.T. had been right, and we had been wrong. I had been thinking of Bitsy as the martyr, but it was the other way around, or, there were no martyrs. Everyone got what he wanted, but feelings were sometimes hurt. Feelings were hurt worst when hurt silently. We knew U.T.'s attitude toward birthdays, but he had not scheduled the reading to ruin Bitsy's. Things just turned out that way. I kept wanting to think of right and wrong like an on-off switch of morality. I was ashamed of having judged so fliply. I finally lifted the fork to my mouth and ate the bite of cake.

Bitsy said,

—When he was younger we both knew how important his writing was, and how he needed to do it seriously. Then all these other things came along—his job, the house, you kids. He's never gotten over not having taken it more seriously, or not being taken more seriously. It's still important to him, but he'll never press it. I forgot. I don't know. Maybe it's best this way. I think Colin understands it better.

She ate a bite of cake. I sipped my coffee. I closed the ice cream carton and took it to the kitchen and put it back in the freezer. Then I returned to the dining room. Before I sat down I took the presents from the buffet and placed them beside Bitsy. The wrapping was clumsy, and though I knew it didn't matter, I was embarrassed. Bitsy reached for a present but I stopped her and sang a brief happy birthday. She clapped and we laughed. I handed her a present, Colin's gift. It was wrapped, patched together, really, in scraps of Christmas paper we had found in the attic. It was the shape of a shoe box, in fact, was a shoe box, with a blouse stuffed inside. To aid the occasion Bitsy shook the package. What could it be, she said. She read the card, a piece of wrapping paper folded and taped to the package. "For Mother, Love, from Colin. Happy 45th." Bitsy tore away the paper bit by bit. when she reached the box she said,

—A new pair of shoes! Just what I needed.

—It's not shoes, I said.

She opened the box and took out the blouse, a dressy white cotton thing with lace around the collar, and held it up.

—It's lovely.

I gave her my present which she opened with equal ceremony. It was the perfume I gave her for any birthday, Christmas, or Mother's Day when she was running out. She thanked me, and dabbed a drop of perfume on her wrists and behind each ear. Then it came time for U.T.'s present. Colin and I had eschewed the store-bought card this year. Instead, we had affixed a folded piece of wrapping paper with the inscription: " '. . . thy eternal summer shall not fade / Nor lose possession of that fair thou ow'st. . . .' Loving you always, Ulysses." For a moment Bitsy sat, looking at the inscription. She looked at me and I looked away. She picked up the racket and tore the paper from the handle and then from the head. It was a very good red tennis racket, strung, as promised, with real gut.

Bitsy bounced the strings against the heel of her hand.

—Tennis, she said. What next?

I began to gather the torn wrapping paper from the table and floor. Bitsy leaned across the table and we exchanged kisses on the cheek,

—Thank you, she said. It was very sweet.

We finished our coffee and together cleared the cups and cake plates.

"I apologize if any of you has heard this before," the readers would say as they stepped to the podium to recite the poems that everyone present had heard so many times before. The same crowd attended each reading in a conference room in the West Bank Union. On this night there was a fire in the fireplace to the left of the podium. There was a good crowd—several of U.T.'s students and colleagues were in the audience. The room was carpeted, with three paneled walls and one wall of glass. As U.T. stood against the mantle he saw reflected in the glass wall the fire, the backs of numerous heads whose faces were trained to the podium, and his own face, looking at the reflections. There was a table to one side with jugs of wine and squares of cheese and plates of crackers, from which the latecomers gathered provisions before sitting down for the reading.

I had been to several readings in this room. I knew the regular cast, the high-spirited but stilted bohemian atmosphere which prevailed, the predictable reactions of the crowd to whatever was read. Tonight, as featured reader, U.T. would be granted privileged status. Most nights he sat among the crowd, the unlettered, unpublished, soul-spewing masses, who came to vent whatever demons pricked them, sent them out of their lush or tawdry rooms on nights like this to sit in the company of what they thought to be kindred spirits, and share small sad fragments of their unreasonable hearts.

But I overstate. On any given night the regulars included one young man with long dirty blond hair, habitually dressed in worn brown corduroy trousers, a purple polyester shirt and a gray pin-striped suit vest, who read what he called "Sexual Sonnets." In fact, they were not sonnets at all, but a dull kind of free verse (if that), lacking rhyme, form, rhythm of even the most banal sort. They were typed in the form of sonnets. One went: "Imagine that you are the Soo Locks, and I am an ore boat. Why imagine? It is real. . . ." He accompanied his reading with rather vulgar gestures of his legs and hips, as if he were utterly enrapt by his verse; this was harder to imagine than his being an ore boat steaming through the Soo Locks. No one seemed to know him, to know even his name. He seemed quite shy as he sat in the rows of folding chairs or stood alone sipping wine after the reading. Sometimes he was accompanied by a small and rather pretty young woman, the Soo Locks, I assumed. He combined the most poignant traits of both the miserable and the naive.

Another of the regulars was an amiable character who read left-wing polemics and crunched cellophane packages of crackers while others read. There were no hard feelings. His name was Blavartsky; he prefaced his recitation with "I am Comrade Blavartsky," and named some regiment of some obscure anarchist-communist organization as his home base. It was generally agreed that he had made this up, which was fine. Blavartsky was round and balding and oily. He wore cast-off fatigues and a field jacket on which he had stitched his name. When he was not crunching crackers he was often traipsing in and out of the room in a less than discreet manner; he had no patience when one of the seated listeners blocked his way. Blavartsky's "poems" were like current events reports from Marxist fairyland. He rendered creative analysis and embellishment of the latest abominations of capitalist imperialism around the world. If a recent event had provoked him unusually he became impatient to have the stage. He could be heard to whimper and grumble, like a puppy waiting for its dinner, as he squirmed in his seat and shredded his cracker packages. He was the pride of the miserable.

There were others, of course, whose cases were less extreme. There were college students whose poetry was sincere, if sentimental and somewhat affected. There were ordinary people from the city at large who for some reason found themselves writing poetry and seeking out other poets. There were professors who attended from a spirit of community. U.T. was among these latter. He took on a fatherly role before the students and poets-at-large who knew him. He harbored a faint hope that all this might come to something, that those who had slighted him in the past, those anonymous people and institutions somewhere east of the Mississippi, might someday take notice and act to repair the damage done. He hoped that his noble actions in the name of literature would someday earn him just plaudits, that his former foes had preserved the memory of the enduring spirit of Ulysses Turner Fraser and would finally grasp the chance to set things right. Or, he just liked going to poetry readings and sharing the company of poets, however flawed. The people who attended the readings knew nothing of his motives. They would not accuse or confront. The room with its fire and wine and literary air was like a safe house.

U.T. always made an occasion of his moments at the podium. Tonight, as featured poet, he had carte blanche. A gesture was surely expected. His repertoire included a few ballads that he chanted with a Beat rhythm, banging out iambs on the podium, dramatic monologues in which he displayed his gift for mimicry, and several meditations on drink and drunkenness that were most effectively read in that state. His best were the seasonal odes, lines on man and nature and their eternal bind. These were his bread and butter. His usual opening line was: "I write Romantic poetry for the Post-Modernist Age."

The student master of ceremonies came to the podium and asked for quiet. U.T. looked at the audience, smiled as he caught the eyes of friends. He noticed Caroline in the front row. She smiled and dipped her chin. U.T. nodded. The master of ceremonies was a young man with short brown hair and small round glasses. He described U.T.'s career, listing a representative few of the many small colleges outside of Boston at which he had taught, and naming some of his obscure publications. Then he gave the floor over to Dr. U.T. Fraser.

U.T. stepped center stage, into the patch of light thrown by a spot overhead. He was dressed in an old black suit with narrow legs and nearly nonexistent lapels. Under the jacket he wore a white shirt with tab collars and a thin red tie. His face was as white as his shirt in the harsh light; he was a black-and-white man, with his blanched face and chest and black suit. The room was quiet save for the crackling fire and a faint rustle of cellophane. U.T. cleared his throat and rubbed his hand against his bearded chin. He began:

—I wrote this first one after seeing the film *Picnic*, from the play by William Inge, with William Holden and Kim Novak. After the movie my son Colin—whom I'm sure you all know— and I ended up in one of those fernbar places, where you see women in glittery sandals and men with gold chains and blow-dried hair. We got drunk and angry about American culture. The poem has an epigraph from the *The Great Gatsby*, where Daisy says, "Do you always watch for the longest day of the year, and then miss it?"

Comatose singer in your hot expensive bar,
stash your gloomy Texas tunes in half-time
Can't you see?
I'm hurting for summer, sadly longing
for hazy sunsets, green evenings
                                    with gin.

Bastard,
Give me a suck of summer,
make me, like Holden
a cruddy Apollo, beautiful, brown, boyish,
with Moonglow and Novak
stepping lightly lakeside.
Then roll 'em:
With damp slugging temples,
a wave of hair,
a blue cotton shirt and shoulders holding night.
One night; a long silver track,
some stones. The curtain drops,
A curtain rises on summer wind,
laden wind from elsewhere.

The audience murmured satisfactorily. U.T. asked for a
glass of wine and one was brought to him. He then read several
short poems on modern themes, moaning and contorting to
make up for what was missing in the lines themselves. The
young poets ate it up, believing that they were having a taste
of the grand old days when poets were men and true men
couldn't help being poets; they summoned the days of the sage-
king. Colin turned to a woman seated beside him and whispered,

—The Mass is entered among us.

The fire burned down. U.T. introduced his series of autumn
poems. These were the hardest for him to write. Though he
celebrated the summer and winter solstices and the vernal
equinox, he let the autumnal equinox pass uncommemorated.
He faded like a consumptive in autumn, though there was
some pleasure in this. I imagined him strapped along the curves

of the earth, spinning sick but happy like a screaming girl on a carnival Tilt-A-Whirl. He was hauled to the center; the axis became his spine and spun him into oblivion. His head pointed true north.

The first autumn poem he read that night was this:

> The graveyard is visible through the trees
> now that the leaves have fallen.
> This ineluctable fall again becomes not a soul.
> The stones on the hill talked stone-speak,
> in the pillared graveyard, among yellow fall flowers.
> I woke from easeful sleep to the rain, cold rain,
> chilling the harvest, turning the oaks to iron
> and flesh to stone. The stones on the hill said, "Winter,"
> the stones said, "Barren, deep, and cold."
> I asked their advice and they said, "Sleep,"
> in stone-speak. I slept, and upon waking,
> I took all the glassware and broke it against the wall.
> I threw a goblet through the window and it fell
> in glassy slivers among the yellow fall flowers.
> The rain drew my window-scene in black and gray.
> The rain said drip-drop and pitter-patter,
> and the stones, ashamed at their loose words,
> fled to a Carmelite rock in the hills
> without a word of thanks or farewell.
> The graveyard was visible all through the winter
> while the leaves of iron oaks mouldered
> beneath the snow and the yellow fall flowers
> dropped their heads in sleep.

U.T. read for forty-five minutes. He ended with Wallace Stevens, "Of Modern Poetry."

> The poem of the mind in the act of finding
> What will suffice. It has not always had
> To find: the scene was set; it repeated what
> Was in the script.
>   Then the theatre was changed
> To something else. Its past was a souvenir. . . .

He stepped down to gracious applause. The stage was thrown open to anyone who cared to read two poems or five minutes, whichever came first. The sexual sonnets poet scurried to the podium and read a new work: "I am a great surging John Deere churning your ripe fields. Is this love?" Comrade Blavartsky had to be asked to leave after holding the stage for seven minutes with an invective concerning the CIA sabotage of the Cuban cane harvest. He packed up his crackers and left in a huff, claiming that he would not be back. Everyone waved good night and called, "See you next time." There were some very bad poems and some fairly good ones; there were poets who were terrible bores and poets who were funny and engaging. The master of ceremonies seized upon the first hesitation among the shy poets who squirmed in their chairs, poems in hand or wadded in pockets, and adjourned the reading. Caroline was among the shy poets. She slipped some folded pages into her backpack. The audience rose stiffly from their metal seats and surrounded the table of wine and cheese. U.T.'s friends greeted and congratulated him. Colin approached him and ceremoniously shook his hand.

—You didn't read the new one, Colin said.

—It wasn't ready. That's my opinion, not the critics'.

—But the critics aren't always wrong.

—True, but the critics are always misguided.

U.T. ended the discussion by pouring a glass of wine and handing it to Colin. They clinked their plastic glasses and drank a toast.

—To the Muse, U.T. said.

—The Muse.

Bitsy's parents telephoned as Bitsy and I were cleaning up the dinner dishes. They were in Arizona for the winter. They called to wish her a happy birthday. They were sorry to miss her birthday, they said, but they would have a party when they came back, sometime in the spring. They asked how things were here, and Bitsy said, cold. It was warm in Arizona, they said. They asked Bitsy to go to their house in St. Paul tomorrow, to check on the plants and make sure the pipes had not burst.

Bitsy hung up, and we went upstairs to the family room. We turned on the television and found an old movie with some notable stars. Though we had tuned in a half an hour late and didn't understand the plot, we left it on. I looked over my homework and Bitsy paged through a magazine. We were both thinking about U.T. and Colin and ourselves, about why we were here and they were there, about why on Bitsy's birthday the house was so quiet and so cold, about why, since everyone got what he wanted, we all felt so bad. I thought it was partly the weather, partly an unfortunate coincidence of events, mostly the irreducible fact of separate lives. Above all it was entirely common.

I had been to U.T.'s readings before, but I had been a guest there, not one of the gang. People asked me trivial questions about school and what I was going to do with my life. It was a burden for them to talk to me at all. When the readings began several years ago, Bitsy had attended faithfully. She had not been a burden. She had been welcomed into the fold; she and U.T. were a lovely couple, wonderful new blood. She enjoyed the readings and looked forward to them. She met new people there and she felt at home. Then what happened? The novelty wore off; the gatherings at bars after the readings became stale and dull; she got tired of bad poetry, of having to digest the half-thought lives of strangers; she got tired of being the less literate half of a lovely couple; the new people never became friends. It was never discussed. Bitsy stopped going to the readings. U.T., of course, kept going. The new people never became his friends, either. He knew many people, but he had no friends, and he kept going to the readings and tonight he was the featured poet and we all should have been there and we were not there and it finally appeared that something was wrong. Maybe it was better this way, Bitsy had said.

For better or worse, this was how it was. Everyone got what he wanted. The attribution of guilt was universal, and the guilt itself thus meaningless. In the worst of possible worlds, where everyone got what he wanted, no one was at fault. U.T.'s aversion to birthdays did have something to do with it. I saw U.T. in a middle ground between calm reality and callous negligence. He made us conscious of the cheap meanings we imposed on meaningless days. We stood between true feelings and artifice. It amounted to a sad lack of communication. If we assumed values in common we were badly deluded. U.T.'s fire-lit reading room was a timeless zone of companionship and communion, or it was artifice, as well. It didn't matter. Only later could we judge, when our various fictions had judged themselves. I wondered which fictions would endure to be judged. U.T. had chosen to neglect commemoration but his tactics would not necessarily succeed. The past made itself over and over. Only the whims of action and memory gave relief to the terrain (I was tempted to think,—the waste land) of the past. Events we would have deemed memorable at the time inscrutably fade, and other moments which on their face bear no omen at all bob brightly to the surface against anyone's will. One could not fight the tyranny of memory. Some scientists said it was all chemical.

I set aside my homework and looked over at Bitsy. She sat in a leather armchair with the magazine open across her lap. Her eyes were closed. Her arms lay on the arms of the chair. I watched her for a moment as she sat with her head upright, her eyes closed. I said,

—Mother, what are you doing?

She opened her eyes and turned to face me.

—Are you still upset about the reading?

She shook her head.

—No, but yes. No, I was trying to imagine what it's like to be blind.

She closed her magazine and dropped it to the floor. She tucked one leg under her.

—There was a blind woman at the museum today. There was a young man with her and he had a note giving her permission to touch the sculptures. He had to go up to the guard in each gallery and show him the note. The guards looked at the two of them as if they were crazy, coming to the museum to touch sculptures. When I saw them they were in a gallery with an enormous statue of a shepherd holding a lamb. The statue was bronze and it must have been seven feet high. The young man showed the note to the guard, then he led the blind woman to the sculpture and she got down on her knees and started from the bottom and felt her way, very slowly, up the whole height of the statue, and all around it; she felt every square inch.

The gallery was empty except for the four of us—me, the guard, the woman and her friend. The three of us stood watching her, very tensely, as if she were defusing a bomb, or delivering a baby. By the time she reached the thighs you would have had to drag me away to stop me from watching. Finally, she stopped. She was reaching as high as she could and her fingertips were on the shepherd's lips. She stood on tiptoe, with her head thrown back, her arms reaching up. She stood that way for not very long, I'm sure, but it seemed like a lifetime. When she took her hands away, the statue changed. It became the one I had seen a dozen times before. Then I looked again, looked very hard, and it started to sink in—all the rough cuts and crevices in the metal, its shape and bulk and how it changed the room. After a short time I couldn't look anymore. The young man took the woman's arm and led her out of the gallery. I went and got my birthday cake.

She stopped and looked at me, then turned and looked at the television. Molly Bloom passed by the door, cast in a suspicious eye and grumbled. As at dinner I was again struck by the impossibility of proper response; I marveled at how expression could tie itself up and seal itself off like some strange artifact on a glassed platform, its sense unclear and all angles of entry barricaded. I tried to lighten the mood.

—So, you want to be blind?

Bitsy gave me a rare motherly look.

—No, dear, I do not want to be blind. I haven't been able to get that woman out of my mind. When I was watching her it was as if I weren't there at all, as if none of us were there— not me or the guard or the woman's friend. It was just the woman and the shepherd and lamb in a great empty space— the way it must have seemed to her. Then later, after I left the museum, I began to wonder what kind of life the woman had— if the young man was her lover, or a relative or friend, or just someone who took blind people to museums. I didn't hear a single word pass between them. I wondered if she was happy, where she lived, if she had a family. She looked to be quite poor.

I thought longer this time before I spoke. I said,

—She might be perfectly happy. She might have friends and parents who love her, and a dog or a cat who doesn't care that she's blind. There are blind people who are happy, there are quadriplegics who are happy. You don't know just by looking. All kinds of people are happy who shouldn't be happy.

I stopped talking. An odd thought came to me, something my English teacher had said about Keats' "Ode on a Grecian Urn." She had explained how the repetition of happy, happy, happy, made happy senseless, make it unhappy, perhaps. There seemed to be some truth in that, but it seemed absurd that you could kill something just by saying it over and over. It was simply that one's attention lapsed. I decided that one must pay attention. Bitsy said,

—I also wanted to know what the woman was feeling when she touched the sculpture, if she had ever seen before and was reconstructing the shape from memory of things seen, or if she had been blind from birth and was making for herself something that we could never imagine. I keep imagining her in a great empty space.

The furnace kicked on, gusting sudden warmth across the room. The house sighed and settled. On the windows in the family room the layer of frost grew thicker as the temperature outside dropped. The crystals piled on top of each other until their delicate shapes were obliterated and the window appeared to be covered in white flock. On the television the black-and-white figures moved frantically to the finale and spoke garbled phrases. Then the news came on in color. I said,

—Is anyone ever really happy? In your opinion.

Bitsy sighed. We had this kind of conversation now and then, when we moved on parallel lines like railroad tracks that seemed to merge but never really met. The record cold was the lead story on the news. Bitsy said,

—In my opinion: Happiness is an absolute. People are more or less happy at different times according to their own measure of happiness and what they want. If one is moving toward what one wants, one might, I think, be considered happy. One must be moving to be happy. Some people convince themselves of happiness by surrounding themselves with material things which they believe to be the manifestations of happiness. Some people turn unhappiness into a strange kind of happiness, or contentment, or resignation. How does that sound?

I nodded, and thought a moment. I said,

—One must keep moving and pay constant attention in order to plot one's course on the graph of life.

—A very nice metaphor. With that, I am going to bed.

I got up and switched off the television. Bitsy said,

—Will you please make sure the front door is bolted? And leave the back unlocked for your father and brother.

I said I would. As Bitsy passed me on the landing she stopped and kissed me.

—Thank you, she said. And goodnight.

—Goodnight, Mother. Happy birthday.

I stood on the landing and saw my full reflection in the tall dark windows behind the staircase. Happy happy birthday. Ah, happy happy boughs! Happy melodist! More happy love! more happy, happy love! I went downstairs to check the doors.

After the reading and the socializing around the wine table the regular bunch, the literate clique, adjourned to Palmer's Bar, a few blocks from the West Bank Union. The gathering at Palmer's was part of the schedule; in fact, it was the main event. Since everyone had heard all the poems (or reasonable facsimiles) several times before, the reading had become something of a formality, a ritual action, if you will, preparing the ground of community and good will whose crop would be reaped at Palmer's. The naive and miserable drifted off into the night and the true literati walked to Palmer's.

The bar was not much to look at, but it filled many needs and drew a diverse crowd from the University and the surrounding neighborhood. The need this night was for a warm and noisy place, a public place for the venting of public sentiment. After glimpsing the slightly sullied world of mediocre poetry, the crowd sought a social setting to clear the air. In Palmer's lay anonymity; everyone became a good fellow and nothing said was taken to heart.

U.T. led the way through the obscure doorway, past the blank façade, into the smoke and noise and warmth of the bar. Even on this Tuesday night it was crowded—a crowd around the pool table, around the jukebox, around the bar. Colin was near the back of the poetic phalange as it filed in. He was talking to Caroline, who had nothing but praise for U.T.'s work. This annoyed Colin, who had learned not to trust Caroline.

—I really liked the one about the movie, Caroline said as Colin held the door open.

—Pap, Colin said.

—What? said Caroline as the door closed.

—Never mind.

The room was long and narrow, with the bar on the street-side wall and one row of unsteady tables and plastic chairs along the back wall. The pool table was near the door, by the cigarette machine, with fluorescent lights hanging above it. The only other lights in the room were two fixtures with tulip-shaped bowls on curving stems at either end of the mirror that ran the length of the bar. The mirror was bordered with an Art Deco wood inlay, its colors faded to light blue and pink. The wood was chipped in spots, showing plaster beneath. At the far end of the bar there were two pinball machines. Several teenagers were gathered around them, shouting obscenities and banging the machines.

U.T. found a table near the pool tables, and the others hustled for chairs. There were nine in all: U.T., Colin, and Caroline; Professor Duncan of the English department; Doris, a woman who published poetry locally; Loraine, a University student and writer; Jonathan, another student who seemed to consider himself U.T.'s protégé; and two of the intellectual toughs with whom Colin sometimes associated. Some of the regulars were missing, stuck at home with frozen cars or simply unwilling to venture into the cold, even for art. Jonathan took orders and went to the bar. The intellectual toughs, Michael and Dante (not his real name), had already installed themselves there and were halfway through their first beers. They wore leather jackets over sweatshirts regardless of the weather, and tight jeans and boots. Dante had short hair left long in front which he had greased into a punkish curl that stuck on his forehead. He and Michael were working on a theory that named Byron as the forerunner of Abstract Expressionism.

Jonathan came back with the drinks, red wine for Doris, ouzo for Duncan, Scotch for U.T. and beer for the rest. When the beer was poured they drank a toast, the second of the night for Colin and U.T.

—To Professor Fraser, Caroline said.

—To the life of the mind, said U.T.

—To Sylvia Plath, Doris said.

—The Revolution, Colin offered.

—Good health, Duncan said.

—Yes, good health, U.T. seconded.

They drank to good health, raising their glasses amid the noise of the pool balls and pinballs, cash registers, the juke box and loud conversation. The table was quiet while they took their first drink. Duncan said,

—I thought the reading went very well, U.T. You really know how to handle a crowd.

Caroline said,

—I very much liked the one about the movie, Dr. Fraser, though I've never seen it, the movie, I mean.

—Oh. Well, U.T. said.

He was reticent only when suspicious. But when he looked over the rim of his glass and saw Caroline, head bowed and face red after her little problem with the antecedent and his own curt response, he softened.

—You really should see it, he said. The movie, if it comes around again. It's wonderful—heat and foreboding, impossible love, lust and romance—the essence of summer. I've seen it a dozen times and I never get tired of it.

Caroline smiled and nodded. Doris said,

—Sounds like a lot of moping and mooning and futility to me.

Doris was something of a pragmatist. She was short and a bit heavy, and her round face was surrounded by short curly black hair. Her skin was oily and she wore wire-rimmed glasses.

—Futility has a lot to offer, U.T. said. It's quite similar to life.

U.T. and Doris usually found their way into a discussion of practicalities and futility at Palmer's after readings, and U.T. always won, because he always managed to lay the burden of proof on Doris, and he could always show that nothing could be proved.

—Art—and literature especially—has a responsibility to action, Doris said.

Doris tapped out "to ac-tion" with her finger on the table. U.T. took a drink of his Scotch.

—Literature, and the thought behind it, have nothing to do with action. They are of wholly different orders. You can, logically, level them to the same ontological status—that of mind, mind reacting to world—but that makes them all useless.

—Beautiful, Doris said. Very neat, very clean. But you're ignoring the fact that things happen, people act on the world, people cause things to happen. There is some kind of hard reality, though maybe we can't quite pin it down.

Doris sat back and drummed her fingers on the table. U.T. took another drink of his Scotch.

—Reality has nothing to do with it, U.T. said. Knowing a little bit about reality is tantamount to knowing nothing at all. It's like guessing at a jigsaw puzzle from a few pieces of the sky. And things do happen, it is true, or seems to be, but the idea of cause-and-effect is pure sophistry. You admit one cause, even a first one, and the world is a machine, the whole of history is predetermined. And dreary old Calvin was right, and so was Borges, who said that God committed suicide in the death of Christ, since He had to know it would happen. Borges also has a nice bit on God's nihilism, based on the assumption that God holds the key to understanding the universe, yet chooses to keep it to himself.

U.T. finished his drink and signaled the bartender for another. He lit a cigarette and sat back in his chair. Doris said,

—God as nihilist. That would appeal to you. But in any practical sense, everything you've said is nonsense.

—I grant you that. I'm just shooting my mouth off.

—And you've committed your own kind of suicide by devoting yourself to the perfection of futility. If you believe what you say, I don't know why you continue. You may have avoided the mechanics of cause-and-effect, but you've given in to anarchy and senselessness. If the world is a machine it must at least have a purpose, but if the world is illusion it is cruel and amoral and a lousy place to stay if you don't have to, which none of us does. It's really quite disturbing.

—Disturbing, to say the least. Certain Gnostics believed that the world was the creation of a minor demiurge, fashioned from a stray ray of light— ". . . a Darkness borne downward, appalling and hateful . . ." No matter what course you follow it leads to futility. There are momentary respites, acts of charity which we feel have redeemed us, but the feeling turns to self-righteousness and pride. So the choice is between safety in abdication which leads to exile and self-hatred or the foolishness of action which we soften with altruism, which leads the same way as the former. There's no way for the waking man to live. I don't know what to do about it. I haven't divorced myself from the world.

U.T. slumped back in his chair. He rubbed his eyes. The wine at the reading and two Scotches clouded his thinking. He looked into his drink and tried to remember what he had said. He knew it was true, all of it, but he couldn't remember why it was so. It didn't make sense as he looked around the room and heard the sounds of music and laughter and pool balls and pinballs. He could not discern the orders of reality present in the room or the ontological status of the bartender, though U.T. knew he must have one, everybody did.

—Divorce yourself from the world? Doris said. Of course you haven't. But you talk as though you could.

U.T. focused his eyes and saw Doris's round face and dark eyes and short curly black hair. She was looking at him with a slightly condescending expression which U.T. did not like. U.T. remembered his college days and late nights in other bars. He remembered other esoteric conversations. He remembered believing that divorcing oneself from the world was the only noble course of action. He concluded that he still believed it. He saw Doris's round face. Pool players were reflected in her glasses. He said,

—You mean I couldn't divorce myself from the world?

Doris looked at him, and her slightly condescending expression changed to one of slight bewilderment. She pushed her small round glasses up on her nose. She said,

—Of course you couldn't. How could you? You're here, we're all here, we're stuck. For better or worse, till death, et cetera. That is reality; that is the fact; that's it.

—I could just ignore it, stop caring. I could go into a room and never come out and stop giving a damn about the world.

—I doubt it.

—You doubt it?

—Yes. You'd have to be crazy, and if you're crazy, it doesn't count.

—Doesn't count?

—No. If you're crazy you're not in this world. It's something quite different.

—You've come around to my side—the world is a fact of consciousness.

—In a sense.

—In a sense?

—Yes.

—What sense?

—Some sense. I don't know.

—Now you're really with me.

Everyone laughed, and U.T. was relieved. He said,

—What can you do? The world exists in some sense and action is illusion and we happened in on the bad part of the dream. Does anyone need another drink?

Jonathan volunteered to get the next round.

Colin was seated across from U.T., facing the pool table. He watched the balls shining in the fluorescent light as they rolled and clacked and dropped down the pockets with a rimming, rumbling sound. The pool players circled the table with cigarettes hanging from the corners of their mouths. They took great care in planning their shots, bending low to see at ball-level, calculating angles with their cues, smoking and thinking. For all that, they were not very good, but they made a good show of barroom eight ball. They shouted and cursed and stomped their boots when a shot failed, which was more often than not. Challengers set their quarters on the table and stood back with beers in hand to size up the competition.

Colin grew bored with the theatrics and took to watching

the balls that were not in play. From seeing where a player intended to shoot, he tried to tell how the other balls would be affected, to plot the probable collisions. After several missed guesses he was able to predict that the yellow one-ball, far down the table from the action of the game, would be pocketed. The yellow one-ball dropped and Colin was pleased. He remembered coming to Palmer's with Marcos when they both were freshmen at the University. Marcos would play pool and Colin would watch. Then they drank beer and plotted strategy. After three beers Marcos became silent and distant. His sharp eyes became dull. Colin was writing and Marcos was failing all his courses. Then Marcos went to Colombia.

Jonathan returned with drinks. Colin turned back to the conversation. U.T. was telling Doris exactly in what sense the world existed. Doris had decided not to agree, but she was not doing very well. U.T. had more practice in describing in what sense the world existed. Duncan tried to help Doris, but she disagreed with him, too. U.T.'s face was red and the scar on his cheek was almost purple. Doris's round cheeks and jowly chin jiggled as she moved her head emphatically. Her glasses bounced on her nose. They were both a little drunk and their mouths moved fast and wetly. U.T.'s rhetoric escalated. He had his elbows on the table and he was leaning over to within inches of Doris's face. She tried to retreat, but Michael and Dante were pushed up against the back of her chair, smirking. U.T. waxed and Doris waned; U.T. had the upper hand and was pressing his advantage, just as he was supposed to do. This was his night.

Colin got up and went to the bathroom. When he came back U.T. had finished off Doris, though no one cared, and the conversation had turned back to poetry, in an anecdotal vein. Colin listened for a while. He watched U.T. gesturing and making faces to illustrate his jokes. Colin looked away from

U.T. and his glance landed on Loraine, sitting next to him. She was tall and thin and pale, with straight black hair cut short and gray eyes. Loraine looked toward Colin just as he looked at her. Their glances locked in an awkward moment. They had been in a writing class together, but had never spoken. Colin smiled with the corners of his mouth. Loraine said,

—Do you write poems, Colin?

Colin was slightly startled. He had expected Loraine to smile back in shared exasperation at the abstruse talk. He had expected the contact to end painlessly, with some small distraction. He said,

—I don't have to write poems; I'm writing poetry all the time.

It was a quotation from Wright Morris. As soon as he said it he was sorry he had, and Loraine was not diverted.

—You sound like your father, she said.

Colin had never been spoken to in this manner. He protected himself from scenes like this.

—Actually, I'm working on a novel, but I want it to be poetic. Shit, I mean. . . . Don't you like my father?

Loraine laughed and turned back to the conversation.

—The poet Yuan Mei was once paid one thousand taels silver for a single funerary inscription, U.T. said.

—Li Po drowned trying to embrace the reflection of the moon on a river, Duncan said.

—How much is that in dollars? Jonathan asked.

U.T. caught the bartender's eye and raised his finger for another round. He was in a fine mood. Doris had dropped out of the conversation. U.T. pulled some bills and a pile of change from his pocket.

—Colin, my son, fetch the drinks, would you? And put some music on the box, songs of innocence for the learned crowd.

Colin rose slowly and took the money. U.T. began another anecdote as Colin pushed his way through to the bar.

I made sure that the back door was unlatched, and locked the front door. I always enjoyed the sound of the bolt snapping fast. All the doors in our house were heavy dark oak, and all had bolts that snapped fast. I went into the kitchen for a piece of cake.

The oven clock showed eleven-thirty. I was sitting in the home of my family, eating birthday cake and drinking milk. It was so very normal on the surface. I imagined the scene through the camera's eye: a wide shot of the house's exterior, quiet and dark, surrounded by snow; move inside to the foyer, and a long shot up the bending stairs; a quick pan of the living room, lingering on the piano and French doors; then a tracking shot back across the foyer, through the dining room, halting in the kitchen door. We see the back of a boy, a young man, sitting at the breakfast bar, eating cake and drinking milk. There's a story here. Who is the young man, and why does he sit alone so late at night, eating cake? Where is his family, and what are they like? Are they happy? (*uh-oh*) but there must be something wrong, or there would be no story. Everyone has heard that old saw.

I wondered what it would be like to have a family I could take for granted. I wondered if anyone did. I knew people at school who seemed hardly to give a thought to the strange notion of families; they engaged in parent–children kinds of activities and had great family fun without the least reservation. Those were the normal, old-time families, traditionalists who had the means to pretend they were traditional. In those kinds of families the children became what they would become, took on careers and got married and produced their own traditionalist families. They went to college at their parents' alma maters and joined the sororities and fraternities to which their parents had belonged. They so enjoyed one another's company, and they could discuss any topic with great seriousness. They knew how people were, how the world worked; or, if they didn't know, they accepted that, too. They loved their parents and their siblings without reservation. Life was sometimes difficult for them, but never overwhelming; everything would always be all right in the end. They could discuss things of the world in profound earnest, without smirking or feeling ever that there was a camera in the kitchen door. Were there really families like that? I couldn't think of any that precisely fit. It was too much television, probably, that made me think in those terms at all. I thought of all the houses, on this street, in this city, this state, on this continent, the millions of houses and the millions of families. What could you say that would even sound true? Maybe happy families were all alike, but the substantiating examples were precious few.

On loving one's siblings: Colin drove me to the airport when I went east to prep school for the second semester of my junior year. I don't know quite how it happened, my going east. I just found myself on an airplane heading for Boston. When I thought about why I was going there, and couldn't come up with an answer, I felt rather silly.

Colin had already begun the novel starring me, *The North Star State*. I had become the model for Gatsby II before the plane left the ground. Colin read parts of it to me. It was full of abstract phrases and uncertain metaphors, and nothing very solid. I was trying to hate him for it, because so much of it was what I thought was true but knew was false. I considered it a kind of faith, believing that phrases like "a Fitzgerald dream of painless union and easeful discovery" do not express things as they are, however much one might like to think in those terms. Colin was exultant, believing that he had the words for the world. His faith was that by knowing the names one could control all things. It was the kind of inanity that comes from university seminars, from reading too much and seeing too little and falling into easy associations. Colin believed that he saw quite clearly the symbolic structure of my journey. He wasn't yet sure how it would end, but he knew it would be something big, heroic transcendence or tragic demise. Fortunately or not, I proved him wrong.

On the morning of my departure we got to the airport an hour and a half early. Bitsy had forced us out of the house before the sun was up, in case there was a line for seating or problems with the baggage or with parking. U.T. was still asleep. He had said good-bye the night before. He shook my hand in a fatherly way, then hugged me. Neither was quite his style. He didn't like good-byes. He gave me a list of people who might remember him and welcome me for a long weekend or a home-cooked meal.

Colin insisted on carrying my bags to the car while Bitsy said good-bye and checked to make sure I had everything I needed. It was early January. In the northern climes, I imagined, all momentous events occurred in winter, as if to defy the glorious monotony of snow and cold. A few cars passed the house on the parkway, their lights on, trailing exhaust, deepening the cold. My hair was still wet from showering and it froze when I went outside. I turned and waved to Bitsy, who stood in the door in her blue bathrobe, a thin tall shape in the doorway, her arm raised and waving, the other arm holding her robe across her chest. My stomach was hollow and weightless. I tasted strong coffee in my throat. I climbed in the car and we drove away.

After checking in and sending my luggage off we still had

an hour before my flight left. We went to the coffee shop and
had coffee and doughnuts. Colin complained about his classes.
He told me about his novel. He was turning the whole thing
around, doing something new with the east–west question,
ringing in a new age of detente. He told me about his new
formulation of the culture/nature opposition, and about Fitzgerald's treason. He was building an indigenous northern style.

We finished eating and there were still forty-five minutes
to kill. Colin bought a newspaper and we shared it, trading
sections. Then we put the paper down. I looked out the window at the crews clearing ice from the runways, at the planes
glittering like ice in the morning sun. Colin reached in his coat
for his cigarettes. He took one for himself, and was about to
put the pack away, then he glanced up at me, unlit cigarette in
his lips, and he extended the pack toward me. He shook a
cigarette halfway out of the opening in the pack. I looked at
him, then at the cigarette. I didn't smoke. I took the cigarette.
I said, "Thanks." Colin rummaged for a book of matches and
lit both our cigarettes. I dragged to get mine going, and I
managed not to cough. Colin leaned back in his chair. He took
a long drag and nodded at me as he blew the smoke out noisily.
I never recovered from the first drag. Each puff was harder to
stand than the last, but I wanted to smoke it well. In a minute
I was dizzy from the nicotine; a minute later I felt sick. We
didn't talk while we smoked—I was too busy trying not to
cough and to settle my queasy stomach. I smoked my cigarette
right down to the filter. When I put it out it was time to board
my plane.

I don't know why I took Colin's cigarette. It seemed the
right thing to do. It was a small thing, but I never forgot it:
Colin offering the cigarette, lighting it for me, the two of us
blowing smoke in the empty coffee shop, like any old morning
in the airport coffee shop. When I boarded the plane in Boston

the next June, going home for the summer and knowing I wasn't coming back to the East, the scene with Colin stuck in my mind like a betrayal, had become, in fact, a betrayal, stony and eternal. It had attained that quality that makes monuments of moments: a stab, a kiss, a cigarette—famous last words. Colin had sent me off into the world, fortified and sustained with the smoke of brotherly love, and I had turned back. It wasn't enough. From the symbol of a cigarette the love drains away and the betrayal remains, fixed and unforgiving, where love had been gentle and fluid, if somewhat awkward.

I sat and ate my cake and drank my milk. In the myriad moments of a family only a few stood out—balloons on a boat, a cigarette in the airport coffee shop. What did they tell me? What *could* they tell me, when each was unique and its sense uncertain? I thought about how my family could be characterized. Certainly it would have to be in U.T.'s terms, because he was the great analyst, the *exégète par excellence*. His terms were the broadest, always coming just to the edge of metaphysical nonsense. He had metaphors galore, and he pushed them as far as he could, to the very edge of dissolving reality, and further, to where the center finally flew away in pieces like the boys and girls wrenched loose from the Tilt-A-Whirl and spinning off into space, out of the colored lights and into the darkness while the carnies watched, astounded, but convinced, nonetheless, that it was bound to happen, and glad, all things considered, that they were there to see it. What a thing to tell. One must pay attention and hold tight. Hold on for dear life, and don't trust your fate to gross mechanics in the hands of minimum-wage transients.

That was one quality of my family: sometimes our metaphors ran away with us. Along with that came the self-critical faculty, a weighty self-consciousness battling the ultimate sense of humor which by its absurdity and essential irony makes everything maddeningly funny. Add to that a distrust of expression, a sense of guarded futility and existential uncertainty which we countered sometimes with reticence, sometimes with fierce loquacity. There you have it: the Post-Modernist family today. In that we were not unique, far from it, but it helped to have a way to think about it. Some glimpse of the way to proper action. Some small hint at making sense. U.T. would say: *Oh! Blessed rage for order, pale Ramon,/The maker's rage to order words of the sea . . .*

Nowadays we have to think that way, even if we don't live it. These were late-night thoughts, the ghostlier demarcations of ill-starred days. One must pay attention and hold tight to the necessary, the necessary balance between involvement and detachment, the maintenance of gross mechanics. The metaphors will catch you every time.

It was now a little after midnight. I heard the rushing sound of the furnace, the electric whirr of the oven clock, the sifting of snow along the top of a drift outside the kitchen window. Outside it was gray, as nights in winter are always gray and never black, with the snow catching any small light. It was gray, too, where I sat, the only light from the upstairs landing giving a gold sheen to the foyer floor and leaving that, shortly, in grayness also. Molly Bloom, our gray cat, paced in from the dining room. Her eyes were blue. She hissed.

U.T. would soon be protesting last call, feigning great distress. Colin would have his coat on and sit impatiently on the edge of his chair, hands in his lap. Was Bitsy asleep, or lying awake, troubled by birthday thoughts? The Post-Modernist family today. I put my plate and glass in the sink and went upstairs to bed.

❧

U.T. finished his last drink as the bartender turned chairs upside down on the tables. Colin sat on the edge of his chair, coat on, hands in his lap.

—It's time, it's time, it's time's wingéd chariot, U.T. said. Why do the bars close so damn early here?

—It's the law, Colin said.

—Never mind the law, said U.T.

Only U.T., Colin, Caroline and Jonathan remained. They had been listening to U.T. expound poetic theory as though he knew what he was talking about. In fact, he did, but it was often difficult to separate the things he knew about from the things he merely talked about as if he did. Finally, when the bartender put a chair on the table at which the four sat, U.T. put on his parka and rose to leave.

On the sidewalk U.T. and Colin parted from the others. Caroline congratulated U.T. once more. Colin was already walking away. Tufts of light snow blew across the empty streets. Colin slowed and U.T. caught up. They walked in silence, hands in pockets, shoulders hunched, to the car. Below, to their right, lay the river iced over save for patches around the pilings of the Washington Avenue Bridge, where the lights of the bridge were reflected. The parallel rows of lights on the bridge led from darkness to darkness, from West Bank to East. The upper row of lights revealed a man on the wide concrete walk.

They passed out of sight of the bridge, behind the West Bank Union where the car was parked. U.T. opened the driver's side door, got in, and let Colin in. Colin sat and felt the cold vinyl chill his thighs and buttocks.

U.T. turned the key and the engine groaned and coughed. After several tries the engine caught. Colin banged his mittened hands together and exhaled a long breath that froze on the windshield. He was still angry about the encounter with Loraine. U.T. waited for the car to warm and the windshield to clear. He turned on the radio. He put the car in gear and drove out of the parking lot past mountains of snow piled at the exit. He said,

—You're not very talkative tonight.

Colin rubbed at the windshield frost with a mitten.

—There was enough talk for a week.

—It's a month till the next reading. We have to stock up.

Colin pushed his hands under his cold thighs.

—I think it's a lot of crap. Those idiots at the reading and those idiots at the bar. It's the same thing over and over. The whole bunch should go into psychoanalysis and try to find out what this traumatic moment is that they have to keep reliving, why they feel compelled to say the same things over and over.

U.T. sighed. His sigh froze on the windshield. He glanced over at Colin, who was staring out the side window. Colin wore a gray watchcap that pushed his straight brown hair down on his forehead. There was stubble of two or three days on his face, and there were several white spots where no beard grew. U.T. remained silent. He pulled on to the freeway that skirted downtown. Colin said,

—It's worthless. It's like doing charity work for people who think they're doing you a favor by letting you work for them. It's completely fucked up. It ought to be worth something, and it's not. Those people will never learn anything, they'll never do anything. . . .

U.T. remembered his college days, late nights when he and his friends emptied many bottles of wine and talked for hours about noble things. He remembered a discussion on the didactic quality of poetry. He remembered falling asleep on someone's couch with a glass in his hand and spilling red wine all over a white shirt. He licked a bit of ice from his mustache. He thought about all that Colin had yet to go through. He wanted to boil down the many years and their few lessons and tell Colin the final sense of it, so he wouldn't be so bitter.

—What can I tell you, Colin? The world is not perfect and those who dwell therein much less so. But just because someone writes bad poetry doesn't mean he isn't trying. Just because he keeps on writing bad poetry doesn't mean nothing has been learned. And even if I'm wrong about that, it means nothing to you. You still have every chance in the world. You've got your whole life to get it right. Don't kill yourself denouncing those less fortunate. Stop coming to the readings, if that's all it takes.

Colin kicked off his shoes and put his feet under the heat vent. He took his hands from under his legs and rubbed his face. U.T. turned off the freeway and toward the lake. Colin said,

—And why do you keep going? A bad poetry reading is a heinous waste of time and a crime against man and God, you always said.

—I stole that line from someone, Galway Kinnell maybe. I don't know why I go. I'm less prone to analysis than you. To share my sense of futility, maybe. Or because I am liked there. If I felt as you do, I would stop going. People learn, slowly, though that's not the point. The point is getting it right. There are hard things to be said, and you must try to say them well. You do it over until you get it right; it's the getting it right that matters, and all else is dross. Effort doesn't count; politics doesn't count; sentiment doesn't count.

They turned on to the boulevard along Lake of the Isles. The trees moved darkly by. The lake was white under a gray sky. Colin said,

—What if you never get one thing right, ever, and you

spend your life failing to say one thing right? Where does that leave you?

—It can leave one in a very sad situation. That is why you should not despise those people who bring their bad poems to the West Bank Union once a month, or anyone else, for that matter. This is a case where effort counts. You have to make allowances for ability.

—So effort only counts when the expression is bad.

—Effort only counts when the case is hopeless. Bad is not bad enough. Hopeless, miserable, and forsaken; that is how bad it must be before one judges by compassion. If it gets so bad that one can only judge by compassion, then the other criteria are meaningless. If you're the only one who knows, you don't know anything. And you can't know anything for certain, anyway, so it's all a sham. That's my trump card—it's all a game in which good and bad are determined by the rules, which we make up. Be proud to be writing fiction.

—And how do you know if you're playing by the rules?

—You know. Slovenliness declares itself in time. You look back, and if there's something there, you know you're all right. Meanwhile, you must try to correct as you go, take nothing for granted, act with consummate humility. There lies happiness.

They passed the big island, and the open patch of water, then turned up the sidestreet to the alley that ran behind the house. The house was dark save for a light in the back hall. U.T. stopped the car. He said,

—That's the main thing: take nothing for granted.

They sat for a moment. The car became cold. U.T. licked his chapped lips. Ice on his red beard rimmed his mouth. Colin said,

—I have one more adage to amend—never leave anything unfinished. Never leave your meaning unclear.

U.T. nodded. He said,

—We're both a little drunk. Here's the last word: he who lives by theory . . .

Colin looked at U.T.

—Dot dot dot? Colin said.

—Dot dot dot.

U.T. opened his door and got out. Colin followed. The cold outside made Colin shiver. The slamming of the car doors echoed down the alley. U.T.'s and Colin's footsteps were loud on the hard snow. U.T. jangled his keys like a night watchman. Colin passed U.T. on the sidewalk and found the door unlocked. U.T. came in behind him. While U.T. stood in the hall unbuttoning his coat, Molly Bloom slipped out of the back bathroom, past U.T., and out through the screen door that did not close into the fifty-fifth freezing night. U.T. did not see her go out. She was not allowed outside in the winter. She was too old. U.T. closed the inside door and checked that it was locked. He turned off the hall light on his way to the foyer.

Colin went to his room. As U.T. passed he saw the light under the door, but said nothing. He stopped in the entrance to the master bedroom. In the grainy gray dark he saw Bitsy's curled shape in the bed. His head throbbed; he rubbed his temples. He felt a sudden sadness at the thought of all these rooms, each with its single occupant, wrapped in blankets, alone and asleep. He whispered to himself,

—And the stones, ashamed at their loose words, fled . . . dot dot dot. I am drunk.

Through the windows across the room he saw the snowy lake and the tops of leafless trees, which seemed to waver slightly. Beyond the trees he saw the dark shape of the island, a black hump, ice-locked. In the window's lower left corner he saw a slice of the open dark water. With effort U.T. caused the objects in the window to become palpable. They rushed into his mind, deep and solid. Quietly, he crossed the room and drew the curtains.

He watched Bitsy breathe as he undressed by the bed. The air pimpled his skin, and his side of the bed was cold when he climbed in. He moved toward the warmth, where Bitsy lay. She was curled with her back toward him. He put his hands on her back to warm them, and she shifted with a small noise. He pulled closer and placed his hand on her breast. She started, gave a short cry, and rolled on to her stomach. U.T. dropped his hand to his side and fell on his back. With his head on the pillow he felt a soreness in his neck. He moved his head and closed his eyes. He went to sleep.

Colin switched on his desk lamp and turned off the overhead light. He sat at his desk and opened his notebook. He wrote:

Marcos remembered the sodden cold mornings that followed the nightly revels with his friends. His friends. How far away that life was, and how regrettable. They had thrown about high phrases as though the world depended on their slovenly utterances, their hackneyed ideas. At dawn they fled from the light, sick and disgusted with their verbal flatulence.

They were ghosts, his friends. For Marcos they no longer existed.

Marcos felt the sun on his face. He smelled the smoke and tasted the bitter coffee and chewed the hard bread. He was no ghost.

When Ramon arrived they would spend a night together with a flask of wine or more, and they would drink in true communion. It would be different, because they were not ghosts.

Ruiz disappeared into the jungle. His mission was evident in his excited gait. He had gone for Ramon, the true Ramon. Marcos happily awaited his coming.

A second day, a second night

❧❧

THE NEXT MORNING was cold again, the fifty-sixth day below freezing. Molly Bloom made memorable the fifty-sixth freezing day. She gave us a way to think about the cold.

Bitsy was the first to rise that morning. She descended the stairs, turned up the thermostat, and went into the kitchen to make coffee. The thermometer showed twenty-five below. As she sat at the breakfast bar waiting for the coffee she heard U.T. in the upstairs bathroom. A moment later she heard him calling Colin and me to rise. I had been lying awake. I had heard Bitsy go down and had waited for the house to warm before venturing out of the covers. I got up quickly when U.T. called and went downstairs before Colin had risen.

I sat in the kitchen and shivered. The radio was on, announcing record lows from all over the state: thirty-two below in Duluth, thirty-six below in Bemidji, forty-one below in International Falls. As Colin had pointed out the night before, it was cold. Colin came in as the announcer confirmed the fifty-sixth day of the freeze.

—Fifty-six days below freezing, U.T. said. A new record. It's just one great day after another. Where will it end?

Colin wiped his sleepy eyes. He appeared not to notice the

milestone announcement, but I knew he had tucked it away in the novelist section of his brain: *When they shipped Marcos home in a plastic bag, his remains unrecognizable, it was the fifty-sixth straight day of below freezing temperatures. A new record. Where he had come from it was very warm.*

Bitsy put bacon in the frying pan and handed the spatula to U.T. She did not like bacon, and she did not like feeling greasy first thing in the morning. U.T. scooped fat over the bacon and hummed "Moonglow," the theme from *Picnic*. The Gatsby poem had planted the seed of summer.

—The reading went quite well, Bitsy, U.T. said. It was a very good turnout, quite a good crowd.

He turned half around and glanced at Colin, but Colin said nothing. He continued to look at the paper. I could see he was not concentrating. U.T. lifted the bacon out of the pan and cracked eggs into the sizzling fat. He put bread in the toaster and when it popped up we cleared the breakfast bar and ate.

U.T. checked over his calendar of literary events. He celebrated Bloomsday with kidneys for breakfast (Bitsy would not cook these, either; she said they made the kitchen smell like a diaper service); he fed the swans on the lake on Shakespeare's birthday; he commemorated the Holy Week of Quentin Compson. Fictional anniversaries were safely celebrated, their significance and purity guaranteed in writing. U.T. had his Romantic poetry class this day. The 155th anniversary of the death of Keats was only a month away, and he was working up something special for that class. The theme of easeful death, fading quietly into the beechen green, was prominent in the course.

U.T. seemed perfectly recovered from last evening at Palmer's. One would have thought that the drinking would take its toll on a man of his age, but instead it was Colin who rubbed at the pain at the base of his neck and cringed at the light. U.T.

hummed "Moonglow." He was thinking about warm damp summer evenings with gin, about light cotton dresses pulled tight on lovely tanned legs by laden wind from elsewhere.

I thought it better to assume a mind of winter. It was not even February, which always seemed like the longest month of winter. There was plenty of time to regret a blithe optimism in the long weeks after groundhog day (which was, incidentally, Joyce's birthday, as well). Even the promise of six more weeks of winter would seem a blessing. Hope of winter's end became reasonable some time in April. February was the longest month, March the snowiest, and April was . . . The adjectives helped to keep things orderly, although bleak. It was better to avoid moral modifiers and stick to the facts, though February was a state of bitter mind. Something was bothering U.T., who had learned to like the cold. He should have been more excited by the record freeze. He kept humming "Moonglow," and his eyes were a little hazy.

Bitsy ate her egg and toast quietly. The remains of the birthday cake sat nearby under cellophane. The wrapping paper lay crumpled in the garbage. The last scent of the perfume that Bitsy had dabbed on last night mixed with the smell of bacon and coffee. It was not entirely pleasant. U.T. looked up from his plate and said,

—You look like hell, Bitsy. You've got those purple bags under your eyes.

—I didn't sleep well. What time did you get in?

—The bars close at one, Colin said. It's the law.

He looked far worse than Bitsy. U.T.'s fork clanged on his plate as he cut through a slice of bacon. He said,

—I'm always ready with bus fare, Colin. I hope you didn't suffer too much.

Bitsy looked at U.T. and U.T. looked at me. Colin lit a cigarette, then reached for the birthday cake and sliced a piece off. He ate it while he smoked. He said,

—Just kidding.

U.T. was still looking at me. He had bags under his eyes too, and his face was pale and the scar on his cheek stood out like a red welt. I didn't like it when he looked that way. He said,

—And you, Bryce, the younger, why so morose? on this historic day, the longest freeze since the advent of meteorology? Buck up, my son, enjoy.

I mumbled something. I said I was tired. I felt stupid. U.T. said,

—Jesus, what a bunch.

I wondered what the night had done to the confused feelings of last evening. Was Bitsy still thinking about her birthday and the reading? How did U.T. feel about half his family missing his big night at the podium? I had thought that by morning it all would be past, and things would continue as usual. We would get on with being a family, such as we were. I thought back to last night's meditations on family. The word had a soft round shape to it, like bread dough rising. It didn't seem to apply. I saw all the wrong attitudes and a refusal of roles, and every kind of denial and negligence. I choked on a swallow of coffee. I thought it might simply be that I was tired, and in a bad mood, and the smoke from Colin's cigarette was making me feel sick. Or, I was just a kid, and didn't understand what was going on, at all. U.T. said,

—Coffee stunts your growth, Bryce. No wonder you both are such runts.

—Leave my children alone, Bitsy said. You're hell on earth in the morning.

U.T. made a slight bow with his head.

—Begging your pardon. These kids are my kids, too.

I motioned for Colin to pass me the birthday cake. He

pushed it across the counter and I cut a piece and put it on my plate in the middle of a pool of bacon grease. U.T. took a piece, too. He said,

—You were supposed to eat the whole cake singlehand-edly, Elizabeth. You've made me a liar to the faces of my peers.

Bitsy apologized.

I couldn't eat my cake. I scraped off the frosting and ate that.

U.T. took one of Colin's cigarettes and lit it.

—Bryce, you look as if you were to die. Have you been drinking behind my back again?

I said I was just waking up. I said I was tired. I was. I said,

—You don't look so great yourself.

—I've a right to look bad, U.T. said. I'm old and a failure. What's your excuse? You are young, but glum.

Then Bitsy changed the subject.

She cleared the plates and put them in the dishwasher. Then she went to the stove and picked up the frying pan. The heat from the stove had melted the frost on the window that looked out on the back walk. Bitsy glanced out through the dripping window. She dropped the pan on the stove.

—My god. How long has the cat been out?

U.T. was off his stool instantly. He beat Bitsy to the door by a step. He opened the door and slowly pushed open the screen. Molly Bloom, who had been leaning against the screen, toppled over, cold and hard. Her fur was covered in gray frost, her body hunched in the shape of sitting. Her eyes were closed as if shut tight against a bright light. U.T. knelt down on the steps and set her upright.

—Oh, Molly, he said.

Colin and I stood behind Bitsy in the door. The warm air from inside gusted out and set the air wavering where it met the cold coming in.

—Oh, my Molly, U.T. said.

Finally he picked her up and brought her in. We retreated to the kitchen. Colin, Bitsy and I stood in a half-circle around U.T., who held the cat before him like an unwanted child. The cat hunched in its final shape as if afraid of being hit.

—Oh Jesus, oh shit, U.T. said, looking at the cat and then at us. What are we going to do? How did she get out? Oh, Jesus, oh, Molly. I'm so sorry.

Bitsy piled newspapers on the counter. She reached to take the cat from U.T. At first he would not let go. Bitsy tugged at Molly Bloom and U.T. let go. Bitsy set Molly Bloom on the newspapers. U.T. stood, dazed and helpless, his arms outstretched.

We stood looking at Molly Bloom. She was a centerpiece on the breakfast bar. A few moments ago we had sat there bickering and joking. The dead and frozen Molly Bloom made me ashamed at the way I had behaved. It was too early in the day for this kind of thing. I looked at U.T. His long arms had fallen by his side, his shoulders slumped down, and he was staring at Molly Bloom. He was thinking hard about the proper and dignified thing to do with his frozen cat. He couldn't think of it. I looked at Bitsy. She was looking at U.T. She was trying to help him think of the right thing to do. U.T. leaned forward with his hands on the edge of the counter. He seemed to have collapsed. Colin went and poured himself more coffee.

U.T. said,

—Well, she's dead.

—Yes, Bitsy said quietly.

On that we could all agree. Bitsy went and poured more coffee for herself and U.T. I went and poured myself more coffee. We stood, drinking coffee, looking at Molly Bloom. The frost on her fur had begun to melt, leaving a puddle on the counter and soaking into the newspaper. Bitsy got some paper towels and mopped up the melt. Molly Bloom sat stately on the counter like an object of worship. We fidgeted around her like uneasy adherents.

Finally Colin spoke. He looked at his watch and said,

—Dad, we've got to get going. I don't mean to be unkind, but there's nothing we can do. She's dead.

—Yes, U.T. and Bitsy said together.

—She's dead, you're right, U.T. said. Let's go.

He threw on his parka and grabbed his bag. He started for the front door, then turned back.

—Are you ready? Colin, Bryce, let's go.

Bitsy went to him in the foyer and took his parka sleeve in her hand. She led him back to the kitchen. She sat him on a stool. She pointed to the cat and in a soft voice said,

—We can't leave her here, Ulysses. She, she's melting. Take her out to the garage. We'll take care of it tonight.

U.T. just sat. He had decided to go, and now he had to think of something else. Bitsy looked at me and nodded toward Molly Bloom. I got a shopping bag and put Molly Bloom, wrapped in newspaper, inside. I took her out to the garage and put her on a shelf. U.T. was slowly coming to himself. We got our things together to leave. Bitsy walked us to the front door. She closed the door behind us, then she found her keys and left the house through the back.

We walked toward the bus stop. Colin and I went ahead of U.T., who was lagging. It was too early in the morning for this, and for U.T. too soon after his dream of summer. Molly Bloom was now a monument to the foolishness of loose hopes.

Bitsy passed us in the car. She honked as she passed. The horn sounded sad. The geese answered. I saw my family marching and driving down the boulevard on a gray winter morning. We had left the house as if evacuated. It seemed to me that people were always leaving our house, often in great distress, and no one ever came in. Whenever people came to visit they never stayed long. From the moment they came in they were saying how they really must go. Even we couldn't stay there. This morning we were emigrés on a gray landscape, or pilgrims in flight from our unexpected idol, the frozen Molly Bloom. We were only going to the bus stop.

From behind Colin and me, U.T. said,

—How long can this cold snap last?

We just caught the bus. The businessmen watched us climb on and guide U.T. to a seat. Even they seemed to guess that something was wrong, that U.T. was in some distress. We put U.T. by a window and I sat beside him. Colin found a seat behind us. The bus rolled away as it did every morning. The businessmen read their papers. I imagined with horror and delight the melting of Molly Bloom, her stately frozen shape sagging like a dissolving sphinx. Then the delight lapsed and the horror remained; I regretted my comment of the night before about putting Molly Bloom down. Someone had to say it, or a crucial element of order and cause would have been lost from our memory of the event. But who knows when one's random remarks will become prophecies? Molly Bloom had given us her cold and placid death. She had died full of faith, I thought, confident to the last that U.T. would be at the door at any moment to let her in and rub off the cold. Or had she lost hope as her old paws and joints froze? Could a cat know despair, recognize the time for final catty thoughts? I hoped that U.T. was not thinking these same thoughts; he was the one that Molly Bloom had waited for.

—I don't know how she got out, U.T. said. I should have heard her. She could yowl like hell, how could I have not heard her?

I was about to respond, offer some kind of comfort, but I had that old feeling, the impossibility of proper response. I nodded instead, and looked out the window past U.T. as the bus turned away from the lake.

※

U.T. and Colin got to the University in plenty of time for their first classes. Colin was scheduled to read from his novel in his writing workshop. He went to the East Bank Union and sat in the downstairs lounge. He paged through the fragments of Marcos. He needed a title for his work. That would lend authority. A good title was important, something telling, but not too obvious, poetic, but clear. He tried to put himself in South America, to feel himself in the steaming jungle. He watched through a sleepy haze as students moved about him. What did he know about South America, or revolutionaries, or Marcos, for that matter? He was here in the frozen north, in the burning, biting, killing cold, where cats froze on doorsteps, and nothing moved for months at a time, and the thought of warmth and ease was desperate. What was Marcos doing in the jungle? What was Colin doing here? What could the waking man do, nowadays?

The noise in the room was a buzz in his ears. He imagined that this could be his hell—sitting cold and still in the overheated basement of the East Bank Union with the buzz of hundreds of students in his ears, sitting there alone and frozen with the pages of Marcos on the table before him.

Colin reached for his paper cup of coffee and took a sip and shuffled his pages. He needed a title. He lit a cigarette. Nothing he could think of had the proper resonance: *An American in Colombia; The Life of a Revolutionary; Death and the Unanimous Jungle.* He wished he had a Bible handy. Many good titles came from the Bible. He needed a simple meaningful phrase. He thought of song titles, he thought of lines from poems. With a father who was a walking anthology he should have been able to think of something.

The crowd of students in the Union began to stir. The buzz grew louder. Colin put out his cigarette and gathered his pages. The crowd flowed out the doorway through a pocket of warmth and the mirage-like curtain of undulant air, into the cold. Colin felt the sting on his ears and nose. He headed for the Washington Avenue Bridge, toward the West Bank and the classroom in a tall building where his workshop met.

There was a covered walkway on the bridge, but Colin walked outside. Through the plexiglass windows of the walkway Colin saw shadowy figures moving parallel with him. He watched the gray band of river ice curve between rocky steep banks. He wondered how far south the ice broke up. At the delta end, he thought, it was warm, the river warm and dirty, fouled with the discharge from factories and slaughterhouses over the better part of the continent. There was always a catch. One thing ran into another, everything was connected. There was a leper colony up every stream.

Colin's right hand, clutching his books, was white and scaly; he had forgotten his gloves in the morning's upset. He contemplated frostbite. Molly Bloom had shown what the cold could do.

The West Bank came nearer, and Colin's hands began to sweat in spite of the cold. He tried more titles: *The True Ramon; Marcos Dies.* U.T. could come up with something, something awfully good. Colin kicked himself for being too proud to ask, but the thought of U.T. gave it to him, one of U.T.'s favorite lines. He had his title: *Hungry Generations. "Thou wast not born for death, immortal Bird!/No hungry generations tread thee down . . ."* Esoteric, venerable, but clean and modern in its context. Colin had never believed U.T. when he said that

Keats was modern. Its implications were many and intriguing—the hungry Marcos, the voracious Ramon, the begotten devouring the begetters, the terrible dynamic of mortality, its profundity and absurdity. Colin felt more at ease as he pushed open the door of the classroom building and went to wait at the elevator.

✌️

—My cat froze to death, is how I am today, U.T. said.

The department secretary had expected nothing so intimate.

—I'm sorry, she said. Have a nice day.

—It's not your fault. Thank you, anyway. She was sixteen, pretty old for a cat.

—I've heard of them living past twenty, the secretary said.

U.T. nodded and went down the hall to his office. From his briefcase he took the sheaf of poems and went to replace them in the file cabinet. He flipped through the pages to see which poems he had not read. He found a recent one that he had forgotten. "Each day the bed of gray ice invites me down." It was a good one, he should have read it. But it was too personal. He put the poems away.

Outside, the fifty-sixth day of the freeze had established itself in gray. It was common knowledge that it never snowed when it was this cold, but U.T. saw a few flakes scrape against the dirty window. Standing by the file cabinet, U.T. looked at the composition of the room. The soft light was soothing. It reached to the middle of the desk then gave way to shadow. There was the jade plant, but the katydid was not in sight. U.T. saw green and gray and brown and pale white. He disturbed the pleasing scene by going to his desk and sitting down.

There was a bundle of ideas in his head. He thought about cats and katydids, the magical speech of old drunkards, endless days of ridiculous cold, a world of adjectives sprung and flung without nouns. That all would have to wait. He had a lecture to give. "La Belle Dame sans Merci" was on the syllabus for today. He had his traditional opening line in mind: "What's all this fairy talk about?" That would get a laugh, but it was not enough. U.T. wanted to lock the door, shove the file cabinet in front of it, spend the day in the soft light and quiet, looking for snow.

He knew that the demise of Molly Bloom would be all over the department by now—another indiscretion. He wanted to blame himself, but he could not. He wanted to be sorry, but what was there to be sorry for? Molly Bloom had been so utterly gone by morning, it was as if someone had removed the real Molly Bloom and left a marble cat statue in her place. She had become a monument to herself. U.T. smiled at the thought. If he knew Molly Bloom she would have liked that.

The bell clattered in the drafty hall. U.T. pulled together his notes and took a deep breath. It was not enough. He did not know what he was supposed to think, how he was expected to act. Act with consummate humility. Say any old thing that comes into your head, indulge yourself in the gesture. They might understand. "What's all this fairy talk about? What ails our knight at arms?"

Bitsy was on the way to St. Paul, to her parents' house, to check for burst pipes and to water the plants. As soon as she got on the freeway she felt that she ought to go home. She missed the first chance at an exit, and she still wanted to go back. She kept driving. She wanted to go back and sit in the cold garage with Molly Bloom. She thought that something important had been forgotten, something obvious that she could not think of. She wanted to do something for Molly Bloom, and for U.T. who was daily being wronged. First the reading, now Molly Bloom. What would tomorrow bring? Things were out of whack, and U.T. was getting the brunt of it. Probably he didn't even know it. Bitsy knew her feeling of dread would pass, when she woke up a little more, and the day got brighter, and she had taken care of poor dead Molly Bloom. But now, as she crossed the river and drove toward St. Paul the feeling was like a premonition of disaster. She knew she could stop it, she didn't know how. The feeling would pass, as feelings always did. But she thought she had been feeling this way for a very long time, longer than feelings ought to last. It was something like how she had felt watching the blind woman. What if they were discovered, she and the blind woman, in that room, that great empty space in the middle of nowhere, she and the blind woman and the shepherd? She remembered the blind woman and the stolid shepherd, and the frightened lamb. She remembered the minotaur and the brilliant girl who led him by his hoary hand. She was the blind woman, or she was the girl. She was the lamb or the dove or the candle.

She drove fast on the gray freeway with its banks of dirty snow. She was into St. Paul and she would not turn back. She got off the freeway and drove through poor neighborhoods toward the mansions of Summit Avenue, a wide street split by a snowy, tree-lined island. Bitsy's parents lived on Summit Avenue in a conspicuous Tudor house.

Bitsy pulled up to the icy curb and got out of the car. She walked up the flagstone steps and stopped at the door to find the key. She wondered why her parents' maid couldn't come in an extra day to water the plants. A great brass lion's head knocker faced her at eye level. She fit the key to the lock and swung the heavy door open on the wide entry hall. She stepped on to the marble floor. The house smelled cold and musty. Bitsy looked around. She stopped and looked. There were streamers and balloons everywhere. Streamers hung from the stairway balustrade and above the doorways leading to the living and sitting rooms. Helium-filled balloons tugged slackly at strings tied to the balustrade, to table and chair legs. Three dining room chairs and two small tables had been moved to the entry hall to anchor the balloons. At the back of the entry hall, near the staircase, was an easel and a card table. On the easel was a flat rectangular package wrapped in brown paper and a red ribbon and a large bow. On the card table, in the middle of a forest of wilted balloons, was a tape recorder and a vase of red roses. Bitsy looked around. All the balloons were slightly deflated and puckered. The streamers that hung above radiators trailed strings of dust. The maid had put them up. So Bitsy did not need to water the plants. But the maid had not been here in several days. Bitsy unbuttoned her coat. She walked across the entry hall to the table and heard her footsteps echo through the house. She stood at the table. She brushed aside a balloon and it came back in her face. With the pen-knife on her key chain she popped the balloon. She popped two more to get to the tape recorder. She bent down to smell the roses. The flowers were blown and the petals dried and brown at their edges. They had very little scent. Petals lay in a circle around the base of the vase. She looked at the tape recorder. A piece of paper taped to it said, "Turn me on!" Bitsy pulled off her gloves and pushed the "PLAY" button.

There was muffled whispering and the sound of someone blowing into the microphone. Then her parents sang "Happy Birthday" with piano accompaniment. Her father's voice came on and began giving instructions. *"Go to the easel and unwrap the package."* The voice paused and Bitsy went to the easel and removed the red ribbon and brown paper. *"It is a Matisse, an original lithograph."* Bitsy saw that it was. A blue woman sat on a green chair in a red and yellow flowered room. Bitsy noticed that the balloons and streamers matched the colors of the print. *"We got it a month ago. The girls at the gallery nearly died keeping it a secret. They're so excited for you."* The girls at the gallery knew that yesterday was Bitsy's birthday. They knew she had lied when she called in sick. Bitsy heard her mother say: *"I know it's too expensive, but our money won't do us any good when we're dead. We'd rather use it while we can enjoy it, to make our daughter happy."* The voice was not on the tape. It was what her mother would say when Bitsy protested their extravagence. Bitsy looked at the print in its plain dark wood frame.

"Now take the envelope from under the tape recorder." It was her mother's voice. Bitsy looked down and saw the envelope which she had not noticed before. She slid it out. *"There are two airplane tickets in there, to Bermuda. You can change the dates to suit Ulysses' schedule."* Bitsy looked at the tickets, the Matisse, the balloons and streamers. The house was cold. She shivered. *"We love you very much and we wish you a very happy, happy birthday."* They sang a final reprise of "Happy Birthday."

Bitsy turned the recorder off. She put the tickets back in the envelope and put the envelope on the table. She walked to the sitting room. She sat in a high-backed chair facing the fireplace. On either side of the fireplace heavy maroon curtains swung down over tall windows. The room was paneled with dark wood. An oriental rug covered most of the wide-planked floor. On the walls there were family portraits painted from old photographs after Bitsy's parents had moved to St. Paul. The old farm folk in the heavy frames had been given sitting room airs in their new incarnations. Everything in the room seemed fake, solid but fake. Above the mantle was a portrait of Bitsy's father's father, her grandfather Carl. Bitsy looked at the portrait, and she tried to remember how Carl had really looked. The painter had removed the marks of weather from Carl's brow and eyes, and had given him a sitting room smile. They—the painter and Bitsy's parents—had dressed him in a dark suit with wide pointy lapels and gold buttons. She would not have recognized him anywhere but in this room. She would not know any of the now dead relatives on the sitting room walls. Their lives had been removed from their faces. History had been reconsidered and solidified in this room. History was now solid, but fake.

On the mantle was a photograph of Bitsy and her parents. The photograph had been taken in this same room, in front of this same fireplace. Bitsy, in a red woolen dress and pearls, sat on the arm of a chair in which her mother sat. It was Christmas, several years ago—that was why she wore red. Bitsy's mother was small and plump and dressed in blue; her hair was faintly blue. Bitsy's father stood behind the chair. He wore a double-breasted gray suit and a red tie. He had small round wire-framed glasses. There was a cowlick on his flat gray hair. The painting of Grandfather Carl rose sternly in the background, in the photograph, and behind the photograph, as Bitsy looked. Those were her parents, her family, and her ancestors hung on the walls. Except that now, in this sitting room, they were no longer hers. It had happened that she and her parents now had different ancestries. Something had slipped, a genealogical mix-up. So what could she expect? The line of descent was askew. Why should her parents think twice about giving her things she did not want, a Matisse and two airplane tickets? They didn't have to think twice, because nothing could change anymore, and their daughter would never grow up, and she would continue to receive their extravagances with the same zeal as that of the high school girl opening pearls at Christmas, the pearls she wore in the photograph, the pearls that hung now around her neck.

Bitsy fingered the single strand of pearls that lay close to her throat on a blue sweater. She looked around the room. She realized how alike the two houses were, ours and her parents'. Maybe that was why people were always leaving our house. Maybe it was fake, too. Bitsy got up. She did not want to stay here and now she did not want to go home. She walked over to a big begonia on the floor near the hearth. She felt the soil and it was dry. She guessed that her parents had told the maid to set up the balloons and streamers on her birthday, but the maid had done it days ago, on her regular day, last Friday. Now it was Wednesday. Bitsy would not tell her parents. She found a watering can in the kitchen and watered the plants. She left a note for the maid. She took down the balloons and streamers and replaced the furniture that had been moved into the entry hall. Then she put the airplane tickets in her purse, she rewrapped the Matisse. She stood at the door with the Matisse under her arm. She did not know where to go. She thought of Molly Bloom in the garage. She thought of U.T., leaving the house as fast as he could because there was nothing we could do. She thought of Colin and she thought of me, and she thought that these were difficult times, the cold gray heart of winter. Very little really had happened. That did not seem to matter. Things were happening all the time that we knew nothing about. It was the cold, and we were all weary.

Bitsy opened the door and stepped into the cold. There was a great quiet on the street of large houses. The sound of her footsteps carried up and down the block as she hurried down the long steps, Matisse under her arm. She got in the car, and as she pulled away she looked back at the house and the dark windows cut by dark curtains and she drove, not knowing quite where.

✼

I was at school with two hours between classes. I went to the publications room where this week's paper awaited paste-up. On a long library table lay the waxed paper sheets with sticky columns of type. There were grainy photographs and headlines and bylines and cutlines stuck randomly over one sheet, like scattered bits of a puzzle, a crazy-quilt of information. My job was to put it all together in an attractive, readable format—no gutters, judicious use of white space, balanced photo arrangement, relief in the gray blocks, harmony in headline size. There was nothing I enjoyed more than creating a pleasing and readable page. The content was predictable. Although the school was a small private one and respected our first amendment rights, there was nothing of much import to write about. We couldn't offend if we killed ourselves trying. So I considered this a formal exercise, something to kill time.

On one wall of the pub room, which we shared with the literary magazine, we had taped the front page from each weekly edition. More than half the wall was now filled with old news. On the end wall was a large blackboard with assignments and deadines written on it. I sat in the armchair we had borrowed from the senior lounge and checked my datebook against the blackboard. The datebook was a present from Bitsy, who did what she could to keep her family organized. The room was cold. I touched the radiator, and it was cold. I didn't expect anything else; there had been no heat in the room all winter.

On my datebook pages for this week I had Bitsy's birthday, U.T.'s reading, newspaper deadlines, hockey practices, glee club rehearsals. There was nothing about Latvians taking over the house, or cats dying, or blind women in museums, or obscure confessions in bars. Just the facts, which were wholly inadequate to any kind of understanding. I wondered why we bothered with them at all. It made more sense to leave the pages blank and fill them in later. That way you could have Latvians alongside cats, *Paradise Lost* and the Soo Locks, blind women and pool players; and it would all make perfect sense. You'd just have to be crazy to try it.

I began the paste-up. My job here was to create the semblance of order. With scissors and Exacto knife and blue pencil I set about compiling another week's poor history. I looked at the sheets of copy, photos and headlines, and a lovely thought came to me. I thought about sending the sheets back to the printer just as they were; let the readers work a little this week, let them find a clue in a cutline and follow it to a photo, to a headline, to the copy. With so many scattered bits the possibilities were myriad. If my math were better I could know if they were infinite, but myriad was good enough. What great joy and confusion there would be! the four hundred-odd-students and faculty wandering about each with his own precious story of the world and its doings, each one sure and happy with his fabulous construction. The proverbial monkeys at their proverbial typewriters would rap out *King Lear* before two stories matched. But then we would be obliged to print a retraction: "The last issue of this paper, we regret to announce, did not represent reality as we commonly choose to perceive it. We are sorry if this most grievous indiscretion placed undue duress upon your sense of order. The basketball game *will* take place at 4:30 this afternoon." The administration would be relieved, and after the crisis the means of ordinary life would be that much more solid.

These periodic crises were healthy things; they threw into relief the mundane course of events and provided opportunities for redirection. In the course of the dulling days our minds drifted and our grasp slipped, and when we finally woke to some loud noise, we did not know where we were or from where we had come. I decided that my revelation of the night before still held: one must pay attention. If one paid attention one might behold all manner of things: blind women in museums, the cat sneaking out the door, the gradual gathering of frost, the demise of a winter city into shimmering fragments. One could behold the entire universe in a perfect turn of phrase or a passing remark. It was all there. I didn't know quite how to go about it, I knew there would be frustrations. U.T. had once read to me the tale of a certain Buddhist who had sat seven days gazing at a bamboo grove, seeking its eternal principle. After seven days he began to feel ill. He went home, exhausted, and decided that the eternal principles were not necessarily to be found in a bamboo grove, no matter how diligently one looked. But if not in a bamboo grove, then where? It had to do with knowing what you were looking at, I thought, which involved preconceptions, so it was all in the head. Alas, always a rub. But if the universe did turn back on itself, as they said, there might be some convoluted, necessarily paradoxical answer. Perhaps the universe was actually spiraling ever inward, curling down in an infinite ingress, inexorably building its centripetal force so that one day—who knew when?—we would be sucked down in a cosmic flush, down and down into a black speck of all matter, bearing the weight of eternity. Then, you knew what you could do with your bamboo groves.

I looked out the window. The parking lot was still there, and so was the snowy hill that rose to an empty lot where a mansion once had stood. From where I sat it did not seem to be spiraling ever inward, but then, the earth did not seem to be spinning itself silly, either, and we all knew it was. I fixed myself on the page-three headlines: "Social Committee in high gear for Valentine's dance." This was how I spent my time, infinite ingress or no.

❧

—O what can ail thee, knight at arms/ Alone and palely loitering?/ The sedge has wither'd from the lake/ And no birds

sing, U.T. read in his best voice.

The class waited for the next line. It was early and they were tired, and outside it was cold. U.T. looked down on a field of heads nodding like sunflowers at dusk.

—What's all this fairy talk about? What ails our knight at arms?

No one responded.

—Take a guess.

A young man in the front row began to raise his hand, then withdrew it, shaking his head. U.T. lit a cigarette and paced the stage. He came to rest leaning against the podium. He smoked. He looked at his students. He saw Caroline in the third row on the aisle, sitting back in her chair, watching him. Someone quietly coughed. Someone cleared his throat. U.T. moved to the side of the podium and put his hands in his pockets and stood, rocking heel to toe, cigarette in the corner of his mouth. He thought that this would be a good day for a short class, skim through the lecture, take no questions, be done and be gone. He returned to the podium and took the cigarette from his mouth. He said,

—You all look rather weary this morning.

Several students looked up, nodded, and smiled. U.T. said,

—But then you look like this every morning.

Several students laughed. U.T. said,

—And you have just enough energy to drag yourselves in here and install yourselves for fifty minutes and write down the bullshit that I dish out. You may take it as the word of God, or you may see it for what it is, but you still come in here and sit and write it down and never make a peep. It's really quite amazing. Do your parents know what goes on here? God, would they be surprised if they knew what went on here. Or maybe they wouldn't. My parents would have been stunned if they'd known what I did in college. Maybe yours wouldn't. They expect you to learn something, I'm sure, so at least they would be disappointed to know that you're not. Or they know you're English majors, so they don't expect you to learn anything. Because, if I haven't mentioned this before, there's nothing to be learned here; at this rate none of us will ever know anything for sure. You'll come out of here not knowing shit. But that's why you're English majors, because you don't want to know shit. If you wanted to know something you'd be in physics, but then you'd go nuts looking for God and universal truth and the basis of humanity behind every damned quark. Quark is from *Finnegans Wake*—". . .Three quarks for Muster Mark . . ." There are hypothetical subatomic particles called charm and grace and beauty. Did you know that? I think that was a lovely idea. We might take this as confirmation of the unity of all knowledge; we might not.

U.T. lit another cigarette and looked at his lecture notes and the typed copy of "La Belle Dame sans Merci" on the top page. He looked out at the class and he saw now not a field of nodding sunflowers but a bed of gray ice. He wished someone would pinch him, or punch him, or put him out of his misery. He said,

—*The latest dream I ever dream'd/ On the cold hill's side.* Our poem today is called "La Belle Dame sans Merci," which the footnote translates as "The Beautiful Lady without Pity." What about that? I myself think that "mercy" would be more accurate, if somewhat more obvious, than "pity." Pity and mercy are two very different concepts, I'm sure you realize. The former is a stagnant and indulgent emotion, while the latter implies an active moral stance, I think, one of the essentials of the human fabric, such as you are supposed to learn in college, and its lack is much more devastating than a lack of pity, which I think is really to be applauded, if one can manage it. Anyway, a better question might be why our *belle dame* should feel either of these things for some strange guy she just met on the old cold hill's side.

U.T. then ran through the tubercular interpretation: Keats' brother died of consumption, from which Keats himself would die—". . . *I see a lily on thy brow/ With anguish moist and fever dew . . .* The curse of the spotted lung." And a sexual interpretation: ". . . the geo-vaginal imagery of, *She took me to her elfin grot,/ And there she wept and sighed full sore . . .*, and we have the withered phallus to go with our spotted lung." He said,

—Keats may have had syphilis. Probably not. Anyway, he was very unhappy about disease. See "Nightingale." Where does true mercy lie? On this earth, or elsewhere? If not on this earth, then where, and what good would it be?

Now he was hitting his stride. His cigarette had burned down to the filter and was about to burn his fingers. He dropped the butt to the floor and stepped on it. He lit another cigarette, and he looked at his students, none of whom had written anything down for quite some time. He leaned on the podium, his long arms dangling over the front of it. Then he stood up straight and ran a hand down his sallow cheeks. And he began to speak again and did not stop for a long time and hardly noticed the students who fidgeted in their chairs like children at church and who were becoming more and more embarrassed the longer he spoke and showed no sign of ceasing. In the thirty-five remaining minutes he told them all that he knew of living and meaning and life in its essential and myriad details, and of the ultimate gravity and meaningfulness of each bewildering particular. He told them they should write this down. He told them how sorry he was that from his life more than twice as long as theirs he could not tell them more things, and better. He told them that this was how it was, that this was things as they were, and the life among them. He described how he had first believed in God, then in poetry, then in neither, because the first was perfect and the second flawed and that, again, was how things were. He could neither believe nor disbelieve in God or poetry, and this was an old problem, shared by many and better than he, and this was some comfort. He spoke of the barrenness of the world, and of its grandeur. He realized it was all nonsense, like talking to strangers on the cold hill's side, and he told them that too.

He brought it down to particulars. He told them about Molly Bloom, his cat who had appeared frozen on the doorstep like an unfortunate orphan. He said,

—My cat is dead and what does it mean? Nothing. I have to tell myself, against all my wishes, that this frozen cat, this pet that I killed, is meaningless. How can I do that? I cannot. No one can tell me that it means nothing, though I know that it is so. Life is a series of excuses and acceptances, pitiful and brave. And who is to judge, and what's the use of it?

He got abstract again and told them about the solitude of the self and sadness and joy all locked up and useless, and everything else that he could think of that seemed more or less true. He stopped. He listened to his fast breath rattling in his lungs, and he felt his hot pulse. He looked down the room and though he knew it was square the illusion persisted of an ever-narrowing column of kinetic space. He was at the flung end of dispersed reality. Then he brought his remarks back to the poem with what he thought was quite a clever move. He said,

—All that stuff about the spotted lung and withered phallus is a bunch of crap, though it may be true. *La belle dame*, this siren, this succubus, is not a woman, but the world. The world will love you to death and you it, in ways you'll never know. If you try to eat weird fairy foods they will not sustain you, though pleasing they may be, and it is never safe to guess at language strange. The poem is about romantic illusions, to which we are all subject, and about the disillusioned Romantic, which is what we are all condemned to be in the disenchanted world. It's about the subjectivity of all knowledge and the treachery of love and existence. It's about floating like a bit of chaff on the winds of eternity, believing you know where you are going. You're always wrong, in some essential way, it doesn't matter, you're always wrong. You have to get used to it.

That was all he had to say, so he stopped, and slumped forward on the podium. He looked at his class. The students sat as if cemented to the backs of their chairs, staring at U.T. as if he had uttered some secret known to all of them but held in strictest taboo. U.T. did not know if the look was awe at his boldness or amazement at his naiveté. And since, because of the irreducible solitude of every inscrutable self, he could never know which it was, he himself was awed and ashamed, and were he granted one miracle he would have asked that he immolate on the stage, or that his class be annihilated and leave him in peace, but since he knew that neither was forthcoming he waited for the bell to ring. And then the bell rang and U.T. said,

—Thank you for your kind attention. You are dismissed.

And though he knew he could never say a sensible word to them again, he said,

—See you on Friday. Read "Ode to a Nightingale."

The students left. Noise and laughter filled the halls and regret filled U.T. He lit a cigarette and stood smoking on the podium until the students for the next hour's class began to enter the room. Then he gathered his notes and he left.

❧

Colin sat in a wooden chair in a classroom six floors up on the West Bank. Through the east windows he could see the river, gray ice under streaks of snow, dark water under the Washington Avenue Bridge. His classmates filed in and sat, and the professor entered, closing the door behind him. The professor's name was Bates; he was a plump, sardonic man who always wore the same gray tweed suit. His face was white and fleshy. Rumor held that he composed his novels by sitting at the top of a flight of stairs and typing anything he could hear of the conversations taking place below. This did not inspire confidence in Colin, who considered himself a rigid stylist. No one knew if Bates had a first name; he was simply called Bates.

For five minutes the class sat, watching Bates as he looked for something in his bag. He gave up and addressed the class.

—Fraser: do you have something today?

—Yes, I have something, Colin said.

—Then let's hear it.

—Shall I tell you about it?

—I know all about it. Read.

—The others don't know about it.

—They'll find out, as soon as you read it.

—It's part of a novel, from near the end.

—You've finished it?

—I wrote the ending first.

—Well. That's too bad. Read it anyway.

Bates jotted on a legal pad as he spoke. Colin sometimes wondered if he copied down all of his conversations for future reference. The thought worried Colin. He wondered if one could copyright one's everyday speech.

—The novel is about a young American who goes to South America to fight for a group of revolutionaries. He worked in the peace movement during the Viet Nam War and became disillusioned with the American conscience. Well, not exactly that. He became frustrated in a more general way, with the way things are . . . here. He's from Minneapolis. But it wasn't just Minneapolis, it was . . . everything. Anyway. It's called *Hungry Generations.*

Bates made more notes. Colin watched Bates make notes and he dropped his typescript on the floor. The class settled in to listen. Colin retrieved his pages from under the table. The floor was dirty. Colin began.

What was death? Death was nothing, nothing but the whimpering nightmare of cowards. Marcos had awakened from that nightmare into a glorious day free of fear. He stood on a high hill and looked down on the unanimous jungle—

—"Unanimous jungle?" Bates interrupted. Did the jungle take a vote on something?

Colin's defense was prepared.

—I intend it in the literal sense, as Borges used it—of one mind.

—Around here we call it anthropomorphizing and, Borges notwithstanding, we don't do that anymore.

Bates waved his hand, a kind of dismissal. He went back to making notes. Colin picked up.

. . . looked down on the jungle, the green-tented land, a mask on the earth. Ruiz was in the jungle; he had gone for Ramon, the true Ramon. Marcos wondered if his courage would fail under the scrutiny of Ramon.

Marcos descended. There was ignominy in this anticipation. Ramon would come in his time, and Marcos had work for his own. As he passed into the trees part way down the hill, he thought: Does the jungle mean death? Is death the meaning of the mask the earth had donned in these latitudes?

Colin read on, and he was sweating, and he read faster. He thought that if he were listening to this, he would not think that it was very good. He thought, in fact, that he would think it pompous and dull. It sounded false to him, all the big easy ideas about death and suffering and rank and file humanity.

He hoped the class would not notice how false it all was. He read faster and sweated more through pieces of dialogue that would have made him laugh if he hadn't felt so sick, since it was he who had written them.

Marcos chastised his men, who had called for a shaman, *brujo*, because something in the wind was not right. Then Marcos went to his hut and made love to Maria, she of the soft brown breasts, whom he could have loved in a different time and place, and he slept and dreamt of the *brujo* like the Narrator pursuing him through the unanimous jungle to the edge of a cliff where he grappled with the black-hatted, red-mouthed *brujo* and they fell, the two of them clutching like lovers, over the cliff and they fell without landing until Marcos awoke.

Colin remembered as he read how Marcos' eyes had not really been wild, but rather sleepy, always bits of sleep in the corners of his eyes, and he talked slowly, not with any authority, but idly. He had worn a beard which stuck out in little spikes that twitched when he talked. Colin's thoughts cleared a great silence in his ears even as he read.

Marcos awoke from the *brujo* dream and made love to Maria again. Colin glanced up and saw his classmates slumped back in their chairs around the long table, yawning and doodling. Bates was still making notes. Colin paused and the class looked up to see if he was done. Colin looked quickly back down to his pages and continued reading. Ruiz came limping out of the jungle as Marcos came out of the hut in a postcoital torpor. Ruiz announced that Ramon was dead, ambushed in the jungle. "Ramon was dead, Ruiz said. All will die, the *brujo* said. Ramon now was dead. All would die. Yes. All." Marcos felt ashamed for indulging in pleasures of the flesh while Ramon was being ambushed in the jungle, but then he thought, that was the way things went. *Que sera, amigos.*

Colin paused at the end of a section. He had been reading

for fifteen minutes, and though he wanted to stop he felt that the only way to save himself was to keep reading. He was about to begin again when Bates said,

—That should do.

Colin straightened his pages and sat back in his chair. He chewed at the end of his pen. He fanned his hot face with his pages.

—Comments? Bates addressed the class.

There was silence, then someone said,

—A little overdone, I'd say.

—Yeah, revolutionaries are really passé.

—Sort of, sort of, gloomy. All that stuff about death and destruction.

Colin rose to his own defense:

—Gloomy? That's the way things are. Death is a fact of life.

—A very cogent observation, Fraser, Bates said, but not very subtle. You need more distance. Put it away for a while. Who's reading next?

Colin stared at Bates, who had now turned his attention to other matters. Colin slipped his typescript into a notebook. Out the window and far below, under the gray day, was the river. The river flowed south and out to sea, and somewhere far beyond that point, Marcos lived, perhaps. Colin glanced at his watch and saw that there was more than an hour left in the class. He didn't know if he could take it.

—This is about something that happened to my family when I was a little kid, the next reader said. It's not very dramatic, but I think it's kind of important. . . .

Bitsy drove through St. Paul on residential streets made narrow by snowbanks at the curbs. She felt like a smuggler with Matisse in the back seat. She thought about the Matisse

and the airplane tickets and the room of balloons and streamers and blown roses and she realized what this was: a gesture of the grandest kind. She almost ran a stop sign.

She pulled over by a park with a small pond cleared for skating. A speed skater slid fast in circles around the pond, his long blades flashing. He was dressed all in black—black skates, black stretch pants, and a black hooded sweatshirt—with his long blades flashing, like Death on ice. A figure skater in a red skating dress and white tights spun on axis in the center of the pond, her head thrown back and her blond hair whipping as she turned tight circles.

In the car Bitsy wondered what U.T. would think of the gesture of the Matisse. Too easy, U.T. would say. It required nothing of the gesture-maker but money and a certain amount of bad taste. Bitsy's parents wound themselves up for gestures at significant intervals; Bitsy thought with a slight panic of what her fiftieth birthday would bring.

A woman and three small children came on to the ice from the warming house across the pond. The woman wore jeans and a long gray coat, and white figure skates. She led the children behind her like a string of ducklings, all holding hands in a chain. The children wore hooded parkas, red, blue, and green, and white figure skates. With the parka hoods up, Bitsy could not tell if the children were boys or girls. They moved in small jerky steps along the edge of the pond. The woman looked back frequently to check on the children stringing behind her like ducklings.

Bitsy watched the woman and the three small children who looked so eager and helpless, in their tiny skates and colorful parkas. She wondered what it was like to be so small and so fragile, a thing we forget. Barely steady on two feet, and they've got you out on the ice. One surprise after another, and it never quite ends. Bitsy knew what the woman, the mother, was thinking. That she had not forgotten. She thought that we had not been skating together for a long time. She remembered how often the four of us went when Colin and I were young. The speed skater passed the mother and her children, going fast, his long blades flashing.

Bitsy thought of U.T., and of Molly Bloom, our cat on ice. The warming house across the pond blew oily smoke up to the gray sky. It was cold in the car. Bitsy looked at the warming house, one small room. Inside the skaters sat on wooden benches and rubbed off the cold, in the heavy warm air like a cell in winter.

The speed skater almost knocked over the mother's third child as he came fast around the curve with his head down. The mother shouted and the speed skater turned backwards and gestured, almost tripping on his blades, and the mother led her children to safety at the edge of the pond. The world was a dangerous place for ducklings and all.

Bitsy left the pond and got back on the freeway. She exited in downtown Minneapolis and drove to her parents' gallery on the edge of the warehouse district. *"The girls at the gallery nearly died. . . . They're so excited. . . ."* Bitsy parked at a meter and sat for a moment, deciding whether to bring the Matisse in with her. She decided she would. She would bring in the Matisse and say nothing about it. That would show the girls.

The gallery was large and bright, with white walls and a polished wood floor. The gallery was quiet when Bitsy came in, and the three older women who worked there—the girls— were standing by the coffee pot at the back of the room. They were talking quietly, almost whispering, though they were alone in the room; they never talked loudly, because of the art. Bitsy did not want to do what she was about to do, but she convinced herself that she had to. She came into the room. The three women looked up. Bitsy said hello. The women said hello, very brightly, as if they knew something, which they did. They all smiled at Bitsy. Bitsy smiled back, and walked, Matisse under her arm, to her office in the rear of the gallery. She went into her office and closed the door, and left the girls to wonder.

Bitsy stayed in her office, four white walls hung with exhibition posters, for a little more than an hour, going over schedules and proposals for shows. Then she left with the Matisse, saying only good-bye to the girls.

❧

U.T. followed the sidewalk back to the English department. The gray light from the gray clouds that had seemed soothing an hour before was now oppressive. A withered phallus? A spotted lung? Yes, and more, rot in every cell, the substance seeping into acid soil where nothing would longer grow. He imagined the words like bricks rocketing from his mouth, his body recoiling after each blast, and his students lunging after the bricks that sailed over their heads or knocked them flying, falling over one another in the aisles. The words like bricks sailed out over the audience and down into a dark chasm beyond the auditorium's blank walls.

He was through for the day. He would get nothing done. On his desk was the pile of papers he had put off grading till today. U.T. sat wearily at his desk and looked out the window. A bed of gray ice and gray speechless stones on the cold hill's side. The sedge had withered from the lake and no birds sang. It all fell together, a shimmering heap. He sat and drowsed, he dozed; last night was catching up on him. From the department lounge down the hall he heard laughter through his door, or echoing through the thin walls. He sat, half-awake, with the laughter and traces of voices like half-dreams, and he was there and half-laughing, he did not quite get the joke. Then he woke. The light changed, or there were footsteps in the hall. The voices and laughter continued from the lounge. U.T. stood and rubbed his long face and pushed back his thin hair. He dropped his arms, angled, at his sides. He had to leave, as clouds passed and the light dimmed, gray, then grayer. He gathered some papers and put on his coat.

In the hall U.T. stopped, the door half-closed. The voices and laughter from the lounge came to him clearly now. He heard his name. A man's high voice said,

—Here we go boys—U.T. Fraser.

Here we go boys—U.T. Fraser. U.T. stopped, leaning forward in the door of his office. What did the speaker mean by that—here we go, boys—U.T. Fraser? He heard other voices:

—Yes, Herr Doktor Fraser.

—Let 'er rip.

He recognized the voices. He could not recall the first speaker's name, but he saw the face—acne-scarred skin and a thin blond mustache, a red bandanna tied over a head of dirty blond hair. He had been a teaching assistant for one of U.T.'s courses. And the cloying Jonathan was there. He had said, "Let 'er rip." The third was named Derek, another of U.T.'s T.A.s, whom U.T. had sponsored for a department grant and who was always very polite.

The bandanna-ed T.A.—his name was Rick, U.T. remembered with satisfaction—cleared his throat and lit a cigarette. He gazed out the window to the black branches of disease-dead elms, and blew out a long stream of smoke. He paused, gazing, and said again,

—U.T. Fraser.

Jonathan laughed, a high laugh, and Derek chuckled, low.

Then Rick began. He spoke in a rough impersonation of U.T. His voice rose from low conversational tones to high-pitched excitement, though he spoke softly, so U.T. could barely hear.

—"What it comes down to, really, what all this shit is about, is that we cannot truly know *anything!* Knowledge, as we conceive of it, is a farce and a fraud, a joke, really, a very, very bad joke, a silly game."

Jonathan laughed high and loud. Derek chuckled, low and smug. Rick paced around the room with exaggerated strides, his cigarette pinched between thumb and forefinger. He made wide gestures with the cigarette hand, and slapped the other hand to his forehead.

—"Eliot, Pound, Joyce, Yeats! What did they know? Nothing! And what is man? A mass of chemical and electrical reactions, a bundle of nerves trapped in his own subjective consciousness, struggling to reach the light, knowing nothing!"

His voice was louder now. Hilarity had fully overcome discretion.

—"I mean nothing—N-O-T-H-I-N-G!"

Derek had given up his smug chuckle and was laughing loudly. Jonathan screeched and choked. Rick, retaining admirable composure, continued. He stood at the window drawn in gray and dragged at his cigarette. Then he turned around and said,

—"I was telling my kids the other day, don't expect easy answers from *me.* I don't have any. There are no answers. God, I wish there were, Jesus.

"And don't talk to me about reality. The relativity—yes the rel-a-tiv-it-y—of all knowledge precludes the possibility of saying anything. That's the futility of language, you know, I'm sure I've told you this before.

"And the futility of poetry. Ah! Poetry! Dear, dirty, poetry!"

Derek's and Jonathan's laughter obscured the monologue.

U.T. strained to hear. Finally, Rick broke, too. Laughing, he concluded,

—"Reality? Reality? Don't ask me. What am I teaching you? What am I trying to say? What? What? Reality? I don't know, who knows? How can we know? It's crazy, it's completely insane!

"Damn, you know, I've been trying so hard not to sound like Eliot."

The three of them laughed and U.T. listened in the empty hall. The laughter came loudly down the hall. Then the laughter began to subside. Jonathan gave regular blurts like sobs. U.T. leaned against the recessed wall by his office door. Derek, short of breath, said,

—Perfect. Absolutely perfect.

He had always been so polite.

—He was going on like that last night at Palmer's, Jonathan said. It was all I could do to keep from laughing.

—It's amazing, the kind of people who get tenure around here.

—I wonder what it's like to live with a guy like that.

U.T., leaning on the wall outside his door, wondered.

Derek said,

—Have you seen his poetry? El stinko. The guy thinks he's John Berryman. A real washed-out beatnik.

U.T. considered the remarks.

A washed-out beatnik.

He wondered if there was any justice in that. He imagined the young faces twisted with laughter and ridicule. He wondered if this was the response to his tirade in class. A good story about ludicrous professors moved quickly through the department. But as a rebuttal it was neither precise nor coherent, and altogether too personal. And, he thought, this scene had probably been rehearsed many times, with more discretion, in various places. It was more a motif than a direct rebuttal. It was random cruelty, children's violence without motive. You could only let it pass; confrontation would be futile.

Then U.T. was embarrassed for the mockers in the lounge. What if he were to step into the door and fix them with a professorial glare? That would be a messy scene. U.T. thought, that would not be fighting fair. There were rules. More than that, he would lose. They held the unassailable fortress of youth, and U.T. himself provided their own best weapon: he was old. Not so old that he would weep for his feebleness once accused, but old enough that any protest would only make him foolish. He could defend himself against any insult or accusation, but he could not deny that he was old and they were young, that he had missed his many chances and they had theirs all before them, though likely as not they would miss theirs, too, and have to face up, as he did, now, and times before, and times to come. It was no use telling them. They would not, could not, understand. And then, U.T. had sought the authority of the bard, not of the elder. He could refute them with a lack of sensitivity or of literacy, but not with their youth. How could he know what they knew and did not know? Keats was dead at twenty-four. The meaning of mercy was hard to know, and imperfect on this earth.

Les enfants terribles sans merci, U.T. thought. He heard a jeering reference to Colin, and to the reading again. The mocking was dying down; they were repeating the best lines: "Damn, you know, I've been trying so hard. . . ." Then there was a lull, and tired quiet laughter. U.T. made his move. He opened and closed his office door, cleared his throat loudly, then started in long strides down the hallway. The quiet laughter in the lounge turned to low conversation. U.T.'s passing form in the door brought down silence in the lounge. He was determined not to look in, but from the corner of his eye as he passed, he saw Caroline sitting on a couch in the lounge. She raised her hand to wave, but U.T. did not pause. They *were* grown devious, all of them.

U.T. slowed after passing the lounge. He tried to catch his breath. The department secretary was out. U.T. scribbled a note and left the building.

On the Washington Avenue Bridge U.T. walked outside and looked north. He saw the lock and dam at St. Anthony Falls a half mile upriver. Water flowed over the dam and fell in a dark turbulent pool that spread out in a half-circle before the ice closed over again. He thought about taking a vacation in the north when school let out for the summer. We could all go up to Superior, he thought, camp along the North Shore, where countless rivers tumbled down the height of land to the lake. We could pick a river and hike upstream until we found a deep quiet pool between rapids, and we could strip and swim and stretch our naked bodies on the rocks. Or perhaps he would go alone and walk into the hills on a pilgrimage. He could settle on a high rock and watch for eagles in their pride of place. He could fast for three days in the heart of the North, where nothing was taken for granted, where everything mattered. He remembered something he had read, it was Kierkegaard on Jesus: "It is not usual to apply the penalty of death for making trivial remarks." He wanted to go to a place where the reverse was true. He would be willing to stand judgment. To the north the river was lost in a maze of bridges. Directly below the Washington Avenue Bridge the river lay in ice, but U.T. saw that it cut through the illusory city to the level of rock and water. The river lay with gravity and made its way in obeisance. Stay low, was the message; everything else would fall. From pride of place in the eye of the sun to the gray light of one's true depths, the ordained decline of all pretenders.

U.T. stopped in a West Bank bookstore. He thought that a good read would set things right. In the magazine section he found a quarterly where his latest article appeared. It was an analysis of "Prufrock," focusing on the image of the scuttling claws: "This is among the most truthful images in all of literature—the poignant 'should have been' of the blind scavenging poet picking at scraps under the weight of the silent sea, the unceasing pressure of an indifferent universe. It is this brutal image of the state of modern man which gives the poem its efficacy. Somewhat later, Eliot found Christ." The words had no impact, elicited no reaction at all. Who cares about a pair of ragged claws? Who cares about Eliot and Christ? Who cares about being right? The wages of trivial remarks, after all, were not death. You could say what you would, and the world would suck in around the vacuum of your words.

U.T. rummaged through the remainders bin and pulled out a book with an intriguing title: *Strange Things Happen Here*. He paged quickly through it. People sat in cafés and eavesdropped; briefcases exploded, or didn't explode; dictators preached from balconies to wet ditches full of the dead. He bought the book and left the store.

On Washington Avenue U.T. caught a bus to downtown. He got off on the edge of the business district and went to another bookstore down a dim side street. The proprietor sold used books under the yellow light of incandescent bulbs on a high ceiling. Shelves of books reached from floor to ceiling all along the walls and in free-standing rows down the long depth of the store to the back where there were no lights. The store was quiet and musty and warm. U.T. heard the owner shuffling somewhere behind several rows of shelves. There seemed to be no order to the books. In one section he found novels, but they merged with books of poetry, which ran into history and foreign language texts. U.T. determined to puzzle it out. He wandered among the high shelves looking for "A." All he could find was the middle of the alphabet, sometimes in order but falling inevitably into a confusion of "B" 's and "W" 's, "G" 's and "R" 's. After a while he gave up on the alphabet and began reading the titles and names of authors. On all the shelves he scanned he saw perhaps a dozen names that he knew. The store seemed like a literary orphanage, a repository of unwanted texts by unknown authors. There were millions of pages and billions of words amassed within these walls, and how many had ever seen the light of a reader's eye? Where did they come from, and where had they gone, these thousands of toilers assigned to obscurity in the dim confines of Levenson's Used Books? Probably most of them were dead, or they sat with their age in gray rooms, witless. U.T. thought that perhaps there lay here, fallow, the talent of a Byron or a Milton, a mind condemned unduly to silence. He might make a grand discovery in this verbal rag and bone shop, emerge from these gray depths with a boon for all humanity, a new light for the world. But where to start? The huge melancholy of the place overwhelmed the thrill of the search. He went out into the gray afternoon, down Fourth Street toward downtown.

It was mid-afternoon when Bitsy returned to the house. Molly Bloom was waiting for her in the garage, frozen, in a shopping bag. Bitsy decided to dispose of her before U.T. came home and had second thoughts about incineration. Of all the ways to lose a pet, Bitsy thought, this was as good as any. No messy writhing on the pavement after being hit by a car, none of the guilt and doubt of having an animal "put to sleep," none of the worry and uncertainty over a runaway. This was good and clean, in its end result, except that Molly Bloom would have preferred not to have died just then, in whatever fashion.

Everyone has to make sacrifices. Bitsy put the car in the garage. As she passed by the shelf with the bag full of Molly Bloom she reached out and gently brushed the bag and whispered,

—Poor Molly Bloom.

Inside, Bitsy looked for a place to hide the Matisse. She slipped the airplane tickets in the kitchen junk drawer, then went through the house looking for an out-of-the-way closet. She found the spot in the back hallway, in the closet there, behind the vacuum and ironing board. So much for Henri, she thought, now for Molly Bloom. Bitsy was alone in the house, but she had the sense of being part of a conspiracy. There were personages all about, visible only to the most discerning imagination. Henri was in the closet and Molly in the garage. The Latvian lady and her swarthy kin waited near the lake for a signal. The blind woman and her henchman with the note, who were now in league with the Picasso lamb-man, had an eye on things, as it were, and would leap into the fray at the appropriate moment. Picasso himself might have joined Matisse behind the Hoover. They were all thick as thieves and as happy and silent as clams. Now that they were assembled, what would they do?

What would they do? What was to become of them? Bitsy put on water for tea and sat at the breakfast bar. The feeling was still with her, that things were all awry. She suspected that when she looked back on these days from the perspective of some years she would remember little, and that of what little was recalled she would think with incredulity, the way one views adolescent embarrassments. She was spending too much time alone, perhaps. She tried to break it down, to get a clearer view. She knew where I was, and that I would be fine, and that Colin would come around, eventually. That left herself and U.T. The subject was so old, so familiar, that it was hard to think about. The kettle whistled. Bitsy got up and poured water over the tea bag in her mug. She sat back down, dunked the tea bag. She pictured U.T.'s face—the high forehead, lightly creased, the green eyes in deep sockets, the long flat cheeks, pinched mouth, red beard with spots of gray. She tried to hear him talking, and couldn't. The face stayed in her mind, but would not speak. The green eyes were soft, sad and weary. Bitsy's hand trembled as she stirred her tea. She stopped stirring. She remembered, she was thinking about something, what was wrong. There was she and U.T., and a problem. Did U.T. see the problem? Was he imagining her face, and trying to make it speak, and trembling when it would not, because he had seen it so many times, for so long? They were in too deep, and had been together too long, to see things clearly, either of them, to think about it, at all. Whatever it was, this feeling, this odd dread—the problem—Bitsy thought, it had been a long time coming. It was not yesterday or today, but a long time. Something like the cold that settled and stayed so long you stopped noticing, so the fifty-sixth day was just a number, like a birthday, an anniversary, something to think about and pretend you understand through the numbers, that you know and feel the many years passed, and the many freezing days. It made for a smooth surface, it saved the appearances. We all knew the appearances were not worth saving, but they kept themselves going, kept us going.

Bitsy looked out the kitchen window. The fifty-sixth freezing day was still there. The thermometer had just edged above zero. She was forty-five years old, and she and U.T. had been together almost twenty-five years. Twenty-five years to arrive at an odd sense of dread. It had been a long waking, so twenty-five years ago seemed like a dream. And what was it like to be awake? An odd sense of dread. You wake, and you remember nothing, you know nothing. You are alone and so is everyone else. You try to come to an agreement on what the world is, what it is like to be awake. All the things you know are of no use; you know nothing and that is solitude. You imagine faces, darkly, and they will not speak. You tremble and teeter like a duckling on ice.

Bitsy wrapped her hands around her mug of tea, and it was cold. The sun was well to the west. The kitchen was in shadow, and cold. Bitsy got up and took her mug of cold tea to the sink. Out the back window she saw the garage, and she remembered Molly Bloom. Molly Bloom's patience was now infinite, but Bitsy did not want her sitting there come spring. She called the vet and her voice sounded strange when she told the receptionist that she had a deceased pet that she wanted to dispose of. The receptionist expressed her regrets and told Bitsy to bring Molly right in.

When the final bell rang to end the day I was in the pub room again. I sat in the big vinyl-covered chair with my feet propped up on another chair. I had been melancholy and listless all day. Part of it was the song that U.T. had been humming at breakfast, part of it was Molly Bloom, part of it was Bitsy's birthday and U.T.'s reading, part of it was the cold. I sat, half dozing, while cold light slanted through the dirty pub room windows, and "Moonglow" ran through my head. I heard the muted horns and the clarinet and the mellow bass. It was impossible not to think of summer with those sounds in my head. And with the gray cold outside, it was hard to find joy in thoughts of summer. U.T. had got it just right with the hazy green evenings, the sense of absolute calm, the damp, expectant hush. There was melancholy in that scene, but it was a compelling melancholy, an elegant despair. I thought that those earlier years had known an elegance far greater than anything my generation would know. It seemed that the world was growing each day a little more vulgar. The rules were being discarded line by line, as if everyone had forgotten the nature of the game, had forgotten, in fact, that it was a game. We piled banality on mediocrity with hungry disregard. The detritus of each failed effort was left to ruin, left to spoil memory.

I heard U.T. humming "Moonglow," and I thought about hazy green evenings. I didn't know quite what to think. There was the intimation of license in the image of the young lovers wrapped in warm arms, dancing slow while the band played in the distant gazebo and the wind carried just enough music to sustain a shuffling sway. There was license in the hazel eyes of the woman who looked up through a wisp of blond hair, who scented her own perfume mixed with sweat and dampness in an odor faint but insistent, who listened to the sound of small waves on the lakeshore, the waves in accord with the soft and distant *plunk, plunk, plunk* of the bass. What could not happen? and what would not be justified? The camera's eye fixes on the stars through a shadowy grove, the music plays, fading, the light fails leaving darkness. Time to lighten the script, undercut the drama. Don't let the audience wander too far unaccompanied.

Then Bitsy entered the picture. I saw her sitting late one summer night in the kitchen. I heard her saying,

—You don't know how many nights I've lain awake waiting to hear the sound of the car in the driveway, the sound of the back door. You don't know how much sleep I've lost over you boys.

I sat with Bitsy at the breakfast bar. U.T. was out somewhere, looking for Colin, who was running with a wild crowd. I was just sixteen, too young to have caused my mother many sleepless nights waiting to hear the car in the driveway, but I was included out of fairness. Colin had just finished an undistinguished first year of college. He was confused and angry about life and his future, which explained but did not excuse his behavior.

—You'll never know how much sleep I've lost over you boys.

I nodded at Bitsy's words, but my attention was focused on the object on the counter in front of me. It was a spiral-shaped piece of aluminum forged in the shape of the large electric burner coil on the stove. U.T. had made it when he went out looking who-knows-where for Colin, and left the pan on the burner and the burner on high. I had come downstairs when I smelled something burning. As Bitsy came in behind me I noticed the frying pan sinking over the burner. The pan had melted clean through. Bitsy burned her hand on the handle as she threw the pan in the sink where it sizzled. I pried the remaining metal from the burner with a pair of tongs and ran it under cold water. Bitsy grabbed the collar of her robe with one hand and looked at the red burn on the other.

We sat down at the breakfast bar. Bitsy talked and I examined the lovely silvery spiral.

—Your father shouldn't let himself be so provoked, Bitsy said. I hope Colin straightens himself out.

My father likes to be provoked, I thought. He thinks that's how fathers ought to be. At that time I still thought of U.T. as a father and not as a problem.

—He tries so hard, Bitsy said. He wants to do what's right for you boys.

He did all right, I thought, though he tried too hard on most occasions. I guessed that U.T., wherever he was, had gotten over his anger by now and realized the silliness of his situation, steaming off into the night in a city of a million people looking for one in particular with no idea where he might be. I imagined that U.T. was now leaning against a tree or sitting on a bench by the lake, smoking a cigarette and trying to think of a way to gracefully return. Most likely he had remembered the frying pan and was watching the house to make sure it didn't burn down. Short of a major conflagration, nothing would bring him back before he had considered his actions thoroughly.

My sleepy mind was drifting around the curves of the aluminum spiral left from the fry pan. I was strangely happy and smug in my knowledge of how it would all turn out and in my certainty of the basic nature of humanity, which was to get terribly worked up over the most pointless things. Bitsy talked and I ran my finger round and round the spiral. At some point we both went to bed.

I didn't hear U.T. or Colin come in, and I don't remember anything more of the incident. It was a run-of-the-mill teenage rebellion made memorable by the incursion of a strange geometry on an unremarkable summer's evening, from dream and myth and the degenerate gyre into our kitchen on Lake of the Isles. More lately I had come to distrust grand symbols with uncertain meaning, but they were useful, I thought, in marking time, if that can be said to be useful. I imagined U.T. smoking down by the lake with a great swirl of galaxy over his head and me in the kitchen with my mother and a piece of contorted metal. If my mind is reasonable I think there is some significance there.

U.T. had taught us to seek universal meaning wherever we might find it. I recalled an incident from the summer past. I had worked as a laborer in a landscape nursery, a family business run by an older couple and their two sons. U.T. encouraged me to take the job. He thought manual labor good for the soul, though he hadn't practiced it recently. Mrs. Kucera, who thought of herself as a matriarch, interviewed me. She asked to see my hands. I thought I'd heard that line in a movie or read it in a novel—*The Grapes of Wrath*, maybe—and it was funny to be hearing it in real life. I showed her my hands. They were, of course, white and soft, barely a hint of callus on them. She made a disapproving noise from somewhere in her throat, and the little hairs on her faint mustache twitched. I sat stolidly; I was now determined to get the job. Then Mrs. Kucera asked me what my father did. I should have said he was a teacher, but before I could catch myself I had admitted that he was a poet. She made three little noises, each successively louder, and her mustache went wild. I told her that Melville had spent time on a whaling ship, Hemingway had fought in every war he could find, and then there was Conrad. I couldn't remember what Conrad had done, but I assured Mrs. Kucera that it was something quite manly. She could see how sincere and determined I was, so she hired me, predicting that I would last two days.

Word got around quickly that there was a son-of-a-poet on the crew. Mr. Kucera was particularly offended, but because he knew how his wife liked to think of herself as a matriarch he couldn't fire me right off. Instead he decided to make me miserable, and in that he succeeded. For two weeks I put up with his constant and abusive scrutiny; I even enjoyed all the attention. Then in mid-June the weather turned hot and business dropped off. There was not much to do but pull weeds. Armed with a short-handled scratcher I crawled up and down the rows of tiny shrubs and trees, tearing the tops off weeds firmly rooted in the hard gray soil. I began to side with the weeds; I admired their survival techniques. And I could have contented myself with such musings, but old Mr. Kucera aptly chose that moment to demoralize me utterly. He followed me up and down the rows, kicking up dust that stung my eyes and clogged my throat, telling me what a poor job I was doing, daring me to quit, or to talk back and be fired. I held my tongue and persevered, just to spite him.

For a week I kept it up, kneeling with dirt and sweat in my eyes, watching the jerky shuffle of Mr. Kucera's Hush Puppies and pant cuffs, while I tore the tops off weeds. On Friday, with an hour left in the week, I decided I had made my point. I got up from my knees and dropped the scratcher to the ground. I looked at the old man. He looked at me. His face turned red. He moved his dry lips soundlessly. I smiled. Then I turned and walked away from him, punched out, and left.

At home I sat on the patio, waiting for U.T. to come home. I was worried about what he would say. At heart an iconoclast, he still believed in good hard work and respect for one's elders. But when U.T. came home and I told him what I had done, I was immediately justified in my own grand gesture. He hugged me and kissed my salty face. He offered to pick up my final check at the nursery. He brought out two beers and we drank a toast to freedom.

—Freedom, he said, is the capacity to perform the only possible, the single necessary action. Cheers.

That afternoon I did indeed feel free. We drank a second toast to liberty and the unvanquishable human spirit. The alcohol sent a fast flush to my face and loosened my thick blood. Bitsy came home and U.T. described with considerable flourish what I had done. He called it "The Great Plunge to Liberty." Bitsy was less impressed than appalled by the way I had been treated, though U.T. exaggerated a bit. Bitsy asked me what I was going to do for the rest of the summer. I hadn't thought about that. I said that I guessed that I would find another job. U.T. and Bitsy went inside, leaving me alone on the patio, the thrill of the Great Plunge somewhat dampened.

Freedom, I thought, my beer mostly gone, was not the absolute I had imagined. It was like bumper cars. You bounced away from one thing and dashed off in an indeterminate direction until you smacked against something else. The sphere of action was severely limited. Freedom was the ability to accept the inevitable—U.T. had that right—and act honestly in its light, but there was nothing heroic or epic about it. You had to prove yourself again and again, explain yourself in full detail, exhaustively, even tediously. There were no footnotes in life. U.T. got me a job researching fairy tales for Professor Teasdale.

From the recollection of the nursery Bitsy again returned. I saw her on her knees in the front flower beds. It was autumn, the sky was gray. Against the rust-colored bricks of the house yellow marigolds were beginning to fade and dry. The gray sky and a light autumn haze sharpened the little color that remained as the air turned cold and the leaves dropped: the rust-red bricks, the yellow marigolds, scattered pink rose petals among the leaves at the foot of a trellis, the blue bandanna on Bitsy's head. She was on her knees, her hair tied in a long curve behind her ears, soiled gloves on her hands. She was putting in bulbs for spring: tulips, daffodils, crocuses, knotty iris tubers. She lingered with an iris root in her palm, turned it over, shaped her fingers around it. In my mind the haze held her there, tall on her knees, her breath drawn up in her chest, her shoulders broad and straight. She held in her hand the rough brown root of an iris, and about her on the moist turned soil lay scattered bulbs of tulip, daffodil, and crocus. Her knees rested in the earth, the bulbs went in the ground, and winter came around again.

The school was empty but the bells kept ringing every fifty minutes. I roused myself from the chair and gathered up my books. Outside it was nearly dark.

Bitsy had walked halfway from the car to the door of the veterinary clinic before she realized that carrying a frozen cat in a shopping bag to the vet's to have it burned might be considered unusual, even suspect. She tried to think of a better way to present Molly Bloom to the vet. She should have wrapped her in a blanket and slouched sorrowfully into the office. She should have thawed her first. There she was, just hours after the death of the family pet of more than fifteen years, toting the unfortunate animal around like a sack of groceries. She hoisted the bag up and held it in her arms. She slowed her pace and put on a look of loss and concern. She rehearsed what she would say to the receptionist.

The office was empty. The receptionist called the doctor as soon as Bitsy came through the door. Bitsy hurried to the counter and set the shopping bag down. She pushed the bag down and pulled away the newspaper in which I had swaddled Molly Bloom, as if to keep her warm. When she had uncovered Molly's head and shoulders Bitsy stood back and dropped her hands to her sides.

—She slipped out last night. She froze to death, I guess. She's still rather frozen.

Bitsy looked to the receptionist for aid and comfort, but the receptionist was alternately staring at Molly Bloom and glancing over her shoulder to see where the doctor was.

—I'm sorry. Dr. Owen, the receptionist called. Mrs. Fraser is here.

—I feel terrible bringing her in like this, Bitsy said. But it's not like this is her at all. I just didn't think.

She motioned at Molly Bloom, then dropped her arm again to her side. Molly started to teeter, and Bitsy and the receptionist both grabbed her.

—Thank you, Bitsy said.

Molly Bloom was still very cold. Dr. Owen finally emerged from the back of the office. He was a tall man with a square head and glasses so thick that his eyes were invisible. He stopped a few steps from the counter and put his hands on his hips. It was very difficult to tell exactly what he was looking at, but his head was directed toward the counter.

—Well, he said. What happened to my Molly Bloom?

Dr. Owen had been Molly Bloom's vet for many years. His attitude reminded Bitsy of our pediatrician; they both managed, without actually accusing, to make her feel that any small malaise or misfortune to her children or cat was her fault. Dr. Owen touched Molly's hoary head.

—My, she's cold, he said.

—She froze to death, Doctor, Bitsy said.

Dr. Owen tapped Molly's shoulder.

—Why, she's frozen right through!

—We're all sick about it, but there's nothing to be done, as you can see. We'd like to have her cremated. Bill us.

Bitsy straightened her shoulders and adjusted her purse on her arm. She decided that she would no longer be victimized by the stupidity that was rampant in the world. Dr. Owen and his receptionist could stand about discussing the frigid condition of Molly Bloom till the cows came home, but Bitsy had seen enough. Dr. Owen looked at Bitsy, and through the wavering depths of his glasses managed to convey a sense of hurt feelings. Bitsy was unmoved. She waited to allow Dr. Owen the last word.

—All right, Mrs. Fraser, he said. I'm very sorry. Hope we see you again.

The receptionist nodded and smiled through her lipstick. Molly Bloom began to tip again, and the receptionist caught her. Bitsy said thank you and good-bye.

�֎

U.T. wandered among the home-rushing office workers downtown. He was practicing an elegant despair, a grand Byronic despondency. The mood was a poetic device that he used to mask his true feelings, which were humiliation and a less elegant, more damaging despair. The Byronic bit had been with him since he was seventeen, in prep school, and he read "Childe Harold's Pilgrimage." He decided that the life of excess and melancholy was the one for him. When he had wandered alone in the New Hampshire granite hills in his moody teens the mask had fit better than it did now, in downtown Minneapolis, as he slouched past a McDonald's and the newly installed Gucci outlet. He had desired to live fast and die young, if die he must, but he had not lived fast enough to gain much attention, and he was now too old to die young. He still imagined, sometimes, that he might finally gain adulation by simply crumbling under the weight of living, the way a child imagines enduring great pain and sacrifice to garner still greater praise in imagined acts of heroism. In the child's mind there still exist the good, the right, and the true, without self-righteousness, with simple faith. Then things change; the world settles in and dies. We settle in, things harden around us. We change our plans. U.T. did not want things to change so. He did not want to settle in and die. He wanted to grow and soar, to be happy and exultant. He wanted to rejoice with full cause. He had not planned on settling for a colorful reputation. His overwrought expectations had become his club foot, forever smacking the doorjamb, thwarting the graceful exit.

U.T. ended his wanderings in the Happy Hour Lounge. He sat at a table and ordered a beer and took out his notebook. He tapped his pen against the rim of his glass. He wrote: "Hundreds of thousands of students are graduated annually with degrees in the liberal arts. Why is there not a perpetual renaissance? Why is the modern world so tawdry and base? Why are we infested with cretins? In my younger days I had dreams of a great and vital community. Am I to be ridiculed for this? Is mockery the price of idealism, or is it something else?"

He took a drink of his beer that emptied half the glass. He read over what he had written. He was dodging the issue. He tore out the page, wadded it, and stuffed it in his pocket. He started again. The bar began to fill up. U.T. kept ordering beers. He wrote:

The course of one's life is essentially random, and it is best to realize this before one gets one's hopes up and makes any plans. If one is cognizant of this randomness, one can prevent oneself from mistaking the arbitrary for the premonitory. Puzzling over ambiguities is futile. Since nothing has significance, ambiguous is merely a euphemism for meaningless.

I love my family, but that hasn't gotten me anywhere. One's kindest actions are received as cruelties, one's sincerest advice mistaken for ridicule or sarcasm. Likenesses are illusory. The dull brain perplexes and retards. The words in which we place so much faith are themselves faithless. Are my children like me? I pray they have more sense.

I took the way I thought was best, not the easiest—far from it. The choice was difficult, or it was simple and inevitable, because I was fit for nothing else. I moved from the hills of Arcady to the halls of Academe, from one cloister to the next, reticent, cowering. I kept myself cloistered, to stay pure and see purely; or, because I was afraid. The glow of purity paled. My cloister was soiled, so I came west; or, I came west because I was out of a job and had two children to feed. One's motives are never clear; or, it is unwise to speak of motives in light of the great randomness. I overcame my reticence and found that there was nothing to say; or, I found that there was far too much to say. There was so much to say that I could not say anything. I didn't believe that the universal was manifest in the particular; or, I believed that line but could not see if it was working. Do I deserve to be ridiculed for this, for not knowing whether there was anything to say? One must believe that there is something worth saying, and I no longer believe it. Then I should just shut up. I am becoming something of a bother. I should have been a pair of ragged claws.

U.T. got up from the table and went to a pay phone near the door. He called Bitsy. The phone rang sixteen times and Bitsy finally answered.

—Bitsy, U.T. said. The phone rang sixteen times. What took you?

—Ulysses? I just got in. I've been at the vet's.

—Come down and have a drink with me, would you?

—Is anything wrong?

—Lousy day at the office. I'm at the Happy Hour Lounge. Bitsy laughed.

—You're where?

—Never mind. I'll meet you at that artsy place on Fourth Street.

—I'll be twenty minutes.

—I'll be wearing a huge gaudy flower.

—I'd know you anywhere.

❧

It was four-thirty and all but dark when I started home from school, and still a few degrees below zero, I guessed. I wrapped my scarf across my face and pulled my hat down over my ears. Only my eyes were visible. I pretended, for a few minutes, that I was a spy, or a downed fighter pilot making my way through enemy territory, occupied Norway, maybe. My disguise was impeccable, my nonchalance disarming. I glanced at the lights in the windows of the large houses; I yearned for comfort, warm bread and mulled wine, but I shouldered my burden and persevered. After about a quarter of a mile I dropped the role on the steep hill of Mount Curve Avenue.

Mount Curve was the street I saw from the pub room window. It topped the largest hill in Minneapolis, and because the city was mostly flat, the hill provided a marvelous view, and so the biggest houses were there.

On the downhill side of Mount Curve there was a large vacant lot where a mansion had stood before it burned. All that remained of the estate was a wrought iron spiked fence running all the way around and the great stone arch over the drive, closed with iron gates. I climbed over the fence to have a look at the view. The lot was overgrown with sumac and small elms, and the snow was deep. I trudged through the snow halfway up my thighs. When I reached the far end of the lot I stepped up on a cross bar on the fence and worked my arms between the spikes. I looked down. I saw the tall city lights and the red taillights of the cars driving west in the dark as urgently as they had driven into the morning sun. I saw the lights of the Mississippi bridges. All around I saw the flat running away to purple sky. A half moon was rising over St. Paul. I was on top of the world, as it was known in these parts. None of the city's noises reached me where I stood; I concentrated on the quiet of the surrounding earth. U.T. often reminded us what was under cities. He lectured on the illusion of concrete.

I remembered when U.T. took us for drives into the prairies toward the Dakotas. We went there often after we first moved to Minneapolis. U.T. had never seen anything like it. He loved to look at the flat, the endless acres of soil and grain as far as you could see. He told us how immigrants from Scandinavia had sometimes gone mad there. All around there was nothing, nowhere to hide from the eye of God, as it was sometimes explained, or nothing to divert oneself from final truths. There was the earth without embellishment. The first settlers lived in little sod houses that were never clean. There was no refuge.

After a while Bitsy tired of driving all day to look at the flat. I don't remember those drives very well, but I imagine that Colin and I were not altogether agreeable, either. So U.T.

began going by himself. He would be gone all day, and Bitsy could never understand how he could stare at the prairie for hours on end. U.T., I decided much later, was practicing a little Zen, confronting the thing that he feared most. The prairie was a void, or a grand mirror, if there was a difference.

U.T.'s day trips continued, and soon it became apparent that he wasn't going only to the prairie. He had widened his range and was now driving anywhere he could drive in a day. He drove not to get anywhere or to see anything specific, but simply to see, to be different places. From these pointless journeys he started bringing things back, small memorabilia of no real value. He brought back pennants, leaves or flowers to dry, stones, postcards, books and ashtrays and China cups and plates from flea markets he had found along the way. He kept them all in a large box in his closet. As far as I know he never looked at them again after he put them in the box, and he put them in with no particular care. At some point he had stopped taking drives. It was several years ago. I don't remember the year. It would seem that he had exhausted the realm of his travels, or lost interest. I wondered if U.T. had lost interest.

I know that at first he was glad to be out of the East. More positively, he liked being in the West. When the train let us off at the Great Northern station, the train's last cars were barely across the river; still, it was west. It couldn't have been Milwaukee, or Chicago, or even St. Paul. It had to be west, west of the Mississippi. U.T. slept most of the way out but woke up to watch the river passing beneath him, to see the West coming on. Out here a man could be his own man, free as the sky, free as a roaming buffalo. There were no boundaries here, none of those New England stone fences that a man needed to keep mending, no more of the smothering hills, the confining sea, the stiff straw men and women. That was how U.T. put it, sometimes, but I never knew whether to take him seriously.

I did know, through subtler intimations, how unhappy he had been in the East. He was out of work in Boston one winter, and it rained from November to March. As the puddles grew larger he would say again and again,

—If this damned rain were snow we'd have a foot.

Then two feet, then three, and we'd be snowbound in his mind and the Scotch would come out. Then he would get started with his polemic on toll roads, historical sights, and Boston drivers. Bitsy ignored him; she said he was just killing time. He got Colin and me laughing so hard we wet our pants.

Of the things U.T. liked about Boston there were the old but unhistorical buildings and the narrow streets, and the way the city had turned its back on the ocean. He liked the street performers in Harvard Square and the air of ferment. In the two or three years before we moved to Minnesota there were politics everywhere and talk of revolution. The talk continued, but U.T. was not there to hear it. It was just as well, since though he liked the talk, he didn't like the people who were talking. Those people were often his students, when he had them.

Most of all, U.T. loved the flashing signs on Storrow Drive:

TRUCK WARNING
Bridge Too Low
TAKE EXIT

TRUCK WARNING
Bridge Too Low
BACK UP

"Too late, too late!" he would moan, and push down the accelerator. "Abandon hope!" He always had us watch for trucks wedged under the bridge, and once we saw one. U.T. was then eternally justified in this view of humanity. Disasters, he said, were to be expected, even the most simply avoidable ones. He was never surprised but constantly amazed by the folly of human endeavor. Conversely, he was able to imagine grandeur in most everything he saw. He leveled all events to the same status through this balance of hard facts and imagination. It was when imagination flagged, I guessed, that he headed west. Bitsy was glad to return, but she saw and knew, even then, that the motive was not adventure or destiny, but flight.

To convince himself that it was not flight, U.T. established a firm residence in his fugitive home. To banish the East from his thoughts, he became a champion of his new home. At first it was out of spite, it was the West against the East, spaciousness and purity against clutter and decadence. In a few years he relaxed that opposition. He began to see, at least geographically, where he was. He called it the North. He became a northerner. He gloried in the cold, in the obstacles that it presented and that were routinely overcome because people must live and endure. He knew, sometimes, that he was living. He knew it when he shoveled two feet of snow from the walk, or when his toes, numb after an afternoon's skating, thawed painfully in front of the fire. That is not the height of human awareness, knowing that one's toes are thawing, but it is a start.

On one of his early drives U.T. discovered Lake Superior and adopted it as his native sea. We passed several summers on its shores. I remember the long exhilarating drive up the North Shore from Duluth to Grand Portage. U.T. had read everything he could find on the history and geology of the lake, and he told stories as we drove, about ore ships wrecked off Castle Danger, the lighthouse at Split Rock, the fortress at Grand Portage, the fur wars and the Indian wars. He told us that the largest mountain on the continent had once stood near the Wisconsin shore of Superior. Migrating monarch butterflies still altered their path to avoid it, like an amputated limb that still hurts long after its removal. He described with high drama the great syncline, the preglacial down-folding of rock that had likely toppled the mountain and formed the beginnings of the Superior basin.

He called Superior by its Chippewa name, "Gitchee-Gumee," translating, "Big Sky Water." He could name all the rivers in sequence from Duluth to Grand Portage as though reciting the alphabet: French River, Knife River, Sucker Creek, Gooseberry River, Split Rock, Baptism, Temperance, Cross River, Manitou, Cascade, and Pigeon on the border past Grand Portage. And as swiftly as saying a rosary he would rattle off the names of the towns: Palmers, Larsmont, Two Harbors, Castle Danger, Silver Bay, Beaver Bay, Illgen City, Taconite Harbor, Little Marais, Schroeder, Tofte, Lutsen, and on. As in his childhood, U.T. had a new cosmos to name and to see. There were the towns and the rivers. There were big things made of rock: Silver Cliffs, Palisade Head, the Sawtooth Mountains. Those were grand things, and knowing their names brought a thrill. The grandest of all, the most thrilling, was the Lake Superior height of land, a phrase that U.T. dearly loved in its transcendent concreteness. The height of land was the volcanic ridge that made the North Shore from Duluth to Grand Portage. The towns sat at its foot, the rivers ran down it. The cliffs and palisades held it up from the lake. It was as old as anything on earth.

U.T. loved to dream all those names and places and things made of rock. He could be there wherever he was, and when he was there he was some place fabulous. He never went there to *do* anything, simply to be there. The lake would not allow much of anything to be done on it. It was too cold for swimming, too deep for fishing, and too big for most boating. U.T. liked that; it contradicted most of the ways one thought about lakes. Within its limitations it was all that it could be. The St. Louis River was its main western feeder; it came in at Duluth. From there Minnesota and Ontario made a tough northern border; the sandy Wisconsin shore and Michigan's Upper Peninsula held it on the south; it ran east to the Soo in the Great Lakes slide, losing itself into Huron. It was a world-class lake if there ever was one. Tops in its field but entirely humble, for all that.

—Call it a lake; it shall refute you, though quietly, U.T. said.

He told us of the misadventures of French fur traders who underestimated the size and power of the lake.

—Can you imagine trying to cross this bitch in a canoe? The Chippewa knew better. The French went stroking out across it and down into the depths singing "Alouette" at the tops of their macho little lungs.

Lake Superior became a kind of aquatic Storrow Drive for U.T. when a house being moved one winter from Bayfield, Wisconsin to Madeline Island fell through the ice. They tried to raise the three-bedroom rambler the next spring but succeeded instead in tearing it to pieces with the cables. On his office bulletin board U.T. kept a newspaper clipping of the house slipping bit by bit through the ice and into the lake, like a torpedoed liner with a peaked roof.

Ice closed the Great Lakes ports in winter. U.T. always watched for the notice of the last ship leaving Duluth, laden with grain or taconite, heading up the lake, hoping to beat the ice. The ice did not keep U.T. away. The lake under ice became still more forbidding and majestically useless, and the lakeshore towns were all but deserted after the autumn color had dropped. We spent Christmas one year in a cabin near Grand Marais. We cut a large Norway pine and stuffed it into the cabin. On Christmas Eve we walked the long piled-stone breakwater around the Grand Marais harbor. The lake had not yet frozen. We sat at the foot of the harbor light and watched the waves. U.T. hardly said a word. This is what I remember best.

On the drive back U.T. pointed out, as he always did, coming or going, the large house on a cliff near Silver Bay. It had been built by the captain of a Finnish freighter who had sailed into Duluth one time and never sailed out. It was a chalet design, and except for its placement unremarkable, but the whole of the pediment under the front eaves was made of stained glass. I had never cared much about the house before. It was a house far away and high up on the height of land, something that U.T. always mentioned in his tourguide fashion. That year I saw it for the first time. I imagined Christmas in that house, the stained glass glowing, the best light on the lake. As we drove past I craned my neck to see out the back window. I watched until the road dropped away and the house was gone. I felt lost and sad. U.T. was quiet again.

My arms had begun to ache from leaning on the fence. The traffic thinned and lights went off downtown. My nose was cold and dripping and my joints were sore from standing so long in the cold. I dropped down from the fence and walked back along the path I had made coming in. When I passed under the stone arch and reached the road I had a feeling of having completed a long journey.

As I walked toward home I noticed the houses again, but differently. I did not pretend to be a stranger or yearn for strange comfort. I tried to imagine the lives inside the houses, because there were millions of lives at large in the world and I wanted to know about them. I was still puzzled by the happiness issue, and I had begun to suspect that I was following a false lead. I was coming to see that my vocabulary was all wrong. It seemed I did not have the words to think about it. I realized, rather sadly, that the people in the houses were not thinking about me. They weren't stopping by vacant lots on snowy evenings, or they were, but wouldn't admit it. Or, they would admit it, but no one ever asked. The real question had nothing to do with happiness. It had to do with our separate lives and with what was going on here. I took some satisfaction from knowing the question.

Meanwhile, I had been walking. I was almost home. There was a light on in the living room.

*

Bitsy found U.T. at a table by a window that looked out on highway construction. There were small square tables in a line along a tall, white, bare wall. The room was dimly lit and small. There was a candle in a glass jar on each table. Bitsy sat down.

—Where's your flower?

—I gave it to a little orphan girl who was on her way to the prom. She was dressed in rags and though she was very pretty none of the boys would ask her on account of her shabby dress. But now she has a huge gaudy flower and I predict she will be the life of the party.

Bitsy smiled and nodded. The waitress came and took her order.

—I had a tea party with Matisse and Picasso, Bitsy said. We plotted something really big.

—I'd like to hear about it.

—Even we don't know what it is. It's extremely confidential. And I went to the vet. Did I say that? I took Molly to the vet.

U.T. nodded. He said,

—Confidentially, I lied about the orphan. There was no flower, either. I've been sitting here listening to all these avant-garde folk chatting about their portfolios, and I am very glad you're here.

—Another hard day in dear dirty Dublin?

—I made a complete fool of myself in class, and the entire English department is conspiring to shame and defame me. I lost my head and delivered a tirade on meaninglessness in the modern world. I got so sick of standing up there, looking into those dull, attentive faces. I felt like I was stealing money from a blind pencil vendor. I just needed to tell them that what we were doing was by any standard useless and possibly damaging.

—Maybe they needed it, Bitsy said. It might have been the best thing you could do for them. I'm sure you overstated the case, a bit, but you must know they expect that from you. That's why they take your classes.

—Yes, it was the best thing for them, but they didn't know what I was talking about. And there's no point in saying it. I might as well have torn up my lecture notes, said, "Aw, shit," and dismissed the class. In all their classes they read about meaninglessness in the modern world. They think it's interesting. I'm wasting my time. If I knew how to do anything else I'd quit right now. I'll probably be fired, anyway. My little exhibition was all that people were talking about.

—You're being ridiculous. You won't be fired. No one will even care. They probably love you for it, anyway.

—Quite the contrary. On my way out of the department I overheard a re-enactment of my lecture, and other assorted slurs, in the department lounge. They think I'm a complete idiot, and I have neither the means nor the desire to defend myself. I just want to hide. How many mistakes can I make?

But that's not it, that's the least of it.

—I'm sure they take off all the professors. They're kids. You need a rest. You're upset about Molly and, things. Call in sick tomorrow.

—Yes, I am sick. A drowsy numbness pains my sense.

—Stop.

—And I don't know if it will pass, alas.

He dropped his head into his hands. Bitsy had seen this act before, but this time it was not all theatrics. She put her hands on top of his and shook his head gently. The waitress approached, then turned away. In the window glass Bitsy saw herself and U.T., going in and out of shadow as the candle flickered.

—Take a leave. You've got tenure, you've been the life of the department. And I've got two tickets to Bermuda. We'll take a vacation.

U.T. lifted his head. He rubbed his eyes. His eyes were red and tired.

—You've got what?

—Well, two tickets to Bermuda and a Matisse, to be exact. From my parents. They planted them at their house, with a tape-recorded message, and balloons and streamers and wilted roses. Their maid set it up, I guess, but a week early.

U.T. was looking off somewhere toward the bar.

—What was that about Matisse?

—They gave me a print, not a reproduction, a lithograph. A genuine Matisse. It's very beautiful.

—And where did you hang it?

—I didn't. I put it in the back closet.

—The closet?

—Behind the ironing board.

—I'll probably just display my ignorance—you were the art major—but isn't that a bit unorthodox?

—It's the latest thing.

She sipped the last of her wine and caught the waitress's eye.

—My parents continue to astound me, Bitsy said. I look at them, and I look at me, and at us, and I simply can't figure out how it all fits. They're like tooth fairies, popping in and out, leaving ridiculous gifts, smiling their tooth fairy smiles. They have raised obliviousness to an art.

She stopped talking and laughed.

—I sound like you, she said.

U.T. looked at her and smiled. The waitress came with another round. She took away the dirty ashtray and left a clean one. The after-work drinkers were clearing out, and the bar was quieter. Bitsy and U.T. could hear themselves clearly now. Bitsy said,

—What's wrong, Ulysses? I can't remember seeing you this down.

—I'm rather surprised, myself. But I think it has been a long time coming.

Bitsy thought, yes, I think it has.

—I fear I have ruined many things. I've turned Colin into a hardened cynic. I've destroyed his faith and his sense of humor. I have nothing to give but morbidity. I feel like some kind of larva, squirming about in a damp noisome cyst. I think that's also called the subjective consciousness.

U.T. lit a cigarette. Bitsy sat with her hands in her lap. She stared into the flame. She said,

—Whatever it is, it will pass. Look around. You can't kill yourself over one lapse in discretion. Whatever you said in class, and whatever you heard, it's not that important.

—You're right. That isn't it at all.

—And Colin is not ruined. He's twenty-one and very smart and pretty mixed-up. That's how most twenty-one-year-olds are. He adores you and he'll be fine. He wants to be a writer and you are the best example he could have. For all your blather about meaninglessness and futility no one ever took his work more seriously.

—Maybe if I hadn't taken it so seriously I wouldn't have sacrificed my better sense. And I wouldn't feel so lousy. Here comes the self-pity. But I never fooled you. Why didn't you stop me?

Bitsy smiled and ran her finger around the rim of her glass.

—Maybe I fooled myself. I always enjoyed your company. I love you, Ulysses.

—And I love you, Elizabeth. O love, O loss. Perhaps I'm making too much of this. It will pass, it should. I don't know. Everything is falling together now. I don't know what to make of it.

—Take some time off. You're only human. You need a rest.

—I think I should get back on the horse, as the saying goes. It's the only way to save face, to salvage my colorful but somewhat tarnished reputation. Maybe next summer I can get a grant, take a leave and write for a few months. And I think we should all take a vacation this summer, together. I was thinking that we could go up to the North Shore for a couple of weeks. That might be what we all need.

U.T. and Bitsy were alone in the bar except for one couple at the far end whose conversation traveled down the room in muffled tones. The patrons' exhalations had frozen on the window, clouding the reflection that Bitsy saw there. Near the candle a patch had melted. In it Bitsy saw the candle and U.T.'s hands wrapped around his glass. She turned and motioned for the check.

—We'll wait till summer if you think that's best, she said. But don't forget there are two tickets in the kitchen drawer. We can go anytime.

U.T. nodded and licked his lips. Bitsy paid for the drinks and they rose to leave. As U.T. put on his coat he said,

—O, for the warm south. If I ever need Bermuda it will be far too late.

—Should I tell my parents that? They'll never take the tickets back.

—We'll send Colin and Bryce on their spring break, have them take lots of slides. Your parents will never know the difference.

Bitsy left a tip on the table and pulled her gloves on. It had become colder since sunset, and the buildings channeled the wind into a steady gust. The half moon was now high over the city. All around were dark warehouses. The wind carried sand and dust from the construction site down the streets toward the heart of downtown. Bitsy held on to her hat. She took U.T.'s arm as they walked to the car. She found her keys in her purse and drove home.

As I came up the walk I caught a glimpse of Colin on the living room couch. A table lamp was on in the living room. The rest of the house was dark.

I put my key in the lock. The cold key stung my bare fingers. I remembered that Molly Bloom would not be there to howl and skulk away when she saw that it was not U.T. at the door. I could not honestly mourn the death of Molly Bloom, but I knew that we would all miss a bit of warmth in the house. Her life had been small, but it was a life, nonetheless, tied up with other lives. For a long time we would look for her in her customary places, forgetting that she would not be there. We would feel sadness, not so much for Molly Bloom, but for not understanding where a small life had gone and why we kept looking for her where we knew she wouldn't be.

I came into the entryway and hung my coat on a hook. The house seemed warm at first, but after I had taken my coat off and adjusted to being indoors I realized that it was quite cold. I checked the thermostat. It was down where Bitsy had set it before she went out. I turned it up. Then I walked back to the living room entrance. Colin was on the couch, staring at the empty fireplace. I said,

—Colin?

He tried to turn his head back to see me.

—Who are you? he said.

—Bryce, your brother.

He seemed to think about that for a moment, then he said,

—Hey, bro.

I went into the room and sat in a chair next to the couch. Colin had his feet on the coffee table. On the end table there was a decanter of Scotch, and several glasses on a silver tray. I looked at the Scotch, then at Colin's eyes.

—Colin, you are toasted.

—Correct. I am invoking the spirit of Scotch whiskey in lieu of the muse.

—Don't give me that crap. What's wrong with you?

—I'll tell you if you have a drink with me.

—I'm not supposed to. I could get kicked off the hockey team.

—I won't squeal on you. Go ahead.

I poured one finger of Scotch and raised my glass in salute. I hoped he wouldn't offer me a cigarette.

Colin shivered.

—Boy, I'm getting the shakes, he said.

—It's not that bad. You just forgot to turn the heat on.

—I thought it was the Scotch.

—Tell me what's going on.

—I'll tell you. It's not that big a deal. I read from my latest opus, *Hungry Generations*, in class today. It was not well received.

—What do you mean? What did they say?

—Someone said revolutionaries were "really passé." Someone said it was gloomy. Professor Bates said to put it aside for a while. He said I needed more distance.

Colin tried to pour more Scotch and light a cigarette at the same time. He dropped the cigarette and a lighted match in his lap. He pounded at the match.

—That's all? I said. That's why you're getting drunk before dinner?

—Reason enough. And I'm not so drunk as I seem, anyway. But I have decided that the political novel is dead. I'm drinking to mourn its passing. It needn't have been so. I never got a shred of encouragement from anyone, not from Bates, not from Dad. Nowhere. I should have been a math major. Linear algebra will never die.

I said,

—Hmmm. Well.

—It's true. Everyone's become so fucking squeamish. "The real world has no place in literature." "All received concepts enjoy equal ontological status." "The physical world is spurious." "History is a fiction." I happen to believe in history. It happened. It's true. People suffer. People die. I believe in the world. Things happen. Things have meaning. The world is more than a bunch of "received concepts."

Colin was more drunk than he would admit. He had gotten himself so worked up he was about to cry. I said,

—People say all those things, but that's not how they live. They don't go around analyzing received concepts all day. They eat, they drink, they sleep, they shit, they fuck.

I surprised myself. I didn't know where all that came from, but it seemed appropriate. I was pleased. I continued.

—You've just got to pay attention and hold on to what you've got. Do what's necessary. Write your political novel. If it's good, it's good. If it's not good, it's not. Either way, it won't kill you. It's only a novel; it's not *you*.

Colin was looking at me intently through a slight haze. I could see that I had surprised him, too.

In the course of my brief monologue I had hiked myself to the edge of the chair and was leaning forward with my hands resting on the coffee table. Now I sat back in my chair, slouched down, and put my feet on the coffee table near Colin's. We both looked down into our drinks. Colin said,

—You're not such a bad kid.

I laughed a little sarcastic laugh, but I knew the compliment was sincere. Sometimes we forgot we were brothers.

Colin seemed more at ease. He drank less hastily. He rubbed his face. He seemed tired. We sat together; neither of us spoke. I wondered if astrology could explain all this strangeness, if there were comets crossing paths somewhere, or a conjunction of distant planets wreaking chaos on our ion fields, or a sudden backspin in the earth's revolutions, or some such thing. Those were easy answers. I remembered what U.T. had said of Colin's first novel, my story. He had said,

—This is paint-by-number fiction, Colin. You've got to forget your myths, forget your collective unconscious and your universal symbols. Get down to the real stuff.

Of course, U.T. was often the last to take his own advice, and Colin, true to his own early training, saw significance everywhere he looked, in all the usual places: in tea leaves and the flight of birds; patterns of cloud and the fall of mute sticks; the grind of the galaxies and the inscrutable path of an electron. These are things one cannot understand, so Colin's fiction was often incomprehensible. But he was true to U.T.'s hopes in looking always for the Deep Hidden Meaning, the beloved

D.H.M. He was no worse than most of us who gleefully accept theories that we aren't willing to live by. U.T. waited on this day of record cold for some revelation; I had sought equivalence in a fry pan gnomon and the Milky Way swirl; Bitsy, who could see, found a virtue in blindness. We did it to get by, I guessed.

I always thought that, looking back, the meaning would leap from the jumbled design and dazzle me with its simplicity, like a *trompe l'oeil* drawing of an old ugly hag in a kerchief that is also a portrait of a lovely young woman at her boudoir mirror. You look and look and all you see is the hag, until someone points out the contours of the beauty, and you slap yourself in amazement because it was there all along. But even looking back, knowing the beauty is there, you hesitate, because what a thing that would be to get wrong. What a gaff it would be to misread your life. Your life. As if it were something you owned, and not something wild and random. Colin didn't even control his own novel. Marcos had taken over since the death of Ramon, the true Ramon, and was running wild through the green-tented land fueled by his paranoid fantasies, dragging Colin along through the underbrush. Marcos should wake up. It has all been a dream. The Narrator is benign.

When I looked at my watch it was almost six-thirty. Colin's head tilted wearily. He had set his Scotch glass down on the coffee table. His hands rested open-palmed by his side. I said,

—You hungry?

He nodded.

—Where are Mom and Dad?

—Don't know.

I got up, took both dirty glasses, and went to the kitchen. I looked for a note from Bitsy. On the memo pad by the telephone Bitsy had written "Huge gaudy flower!!" and underlined it twice. That was a nice thing to find when one was concerned about the whereabouts of one's parents. I sat down on a stool and started to laugh. Colin came in, walking slowly and unsteadily.

—What's so funny?

I showed him the memo pad. He looked at it, then dropped it on the counter. He didn't get the joke. He took a stool across from me at the breakfast bar. I sensed that the respect I had gained just a few minutes earlier had suddenly dissipated. I stopped laughing and went to the refrigerator. I found a package of ground beef and set it on the counter. I said,

—Sorry, I came in here and found this note, and I started laughing and I couldn't stop.

—Sure.

—I don't know why it seemed so funny.

Colin managed a small smile. He drew a circle around the words on the memo pad.

—Huge gaudy flower, he said. I wonder what that means.

—It's horribly overwritten.

—Yes, and too ambiguous. She should have named the flower. The adjectives aren't very descriptive.

—Maybe it's parody.

—Maybe, but if so she should have made that clear.

Colin drew parentheses around the circle and wrote "dele" in the upper right-hand margin. I made two hamburgers and put them under the broiler. A sense of humor was a wonderful thing to have, I thought. If you could perform textual exegesis on a cryptic notepad jotting, I guessed you were all right.

We heard a car in the alley, then saw the headlights flash through the garage windows. I took out the ground beef again and made two more hamburgers. Through the kitchen window I saw Bitsy come from the garage and on to the back walk. She stopped and looked back for U.T., who followed her out and closed the door behind him. Bitsy reached around U.T.'s neck and kissed his cheek. Then he took her arm and they walked, arm-in-arm, up the short walk to the house.

We sat around the breakfast bar eating hamburgers and potato chips. I expected some invective from U.T. regarding the plebeian repast, but he just ate. Bitsy was eyeing him all through dinner. Colin took little bites of his hamburger and fixed his eyes on his plate. He was sliding into an early-evening hangover. I had forgotten all about the huge gaudy flower.

Halfway through dinner U.T. put down his hamburger and leaned forward on the counter. He glanced around the counter and cleared his throat to gain our attention. After a moment of silence he said,

—Your mother and I have been talking about taking a vacation this summer, all of us, together. After school lets out, and before you start your summer jobs, I think, we think, it would be very nice if we went up north for a week or two. We could camp along the North Shore, and do some backpacking in the height of land. Since we haven't had a family vacation for quite a while, and since both of you will be completing your respective senior years and going off to who-knows-where, I think it would be most appropriate if we took this opportunity to spend some time together. One of the English faculty told me about a spot on the Temperance River, a couple of miles from the lake, where there's a waterfall and a pool below it. You can ride right over the falls and down into the pool without a scratch. We could do some fishing, too. The steelhead will be running. Do you remember what fresh-caught trout is like for breakfast? Of all the good places along the lake and up in the height, my friend said, this is the best good place. Not far from the falls there's a great mass of rock, and if you climb to the top of it you can see the lake. You can see the lights of ore ships passing at night, and the breakwater light at Grand Marais. It's illegal to camp there, of course, but it's so far up the river that no one ever goes there. And if we wanted, we could hike even farther inland, over the height and into the Boundary Waters. There are so many absolutely pristine lakes there, we'd have trouble choosing. The walleye fishing in some of those lakes is incredible.

He stopped, shaking his head in disbelief at the walleye fishing in some of those lakes. This was some kind of hard sell. Everyone in Minnesota knew about the Boundary Waters, its pristine lakes and the walleye fishing. None of us responded. U.T. said,

—What do you think?

Bitsy smiled at us. "Say yes, with vigor," the smile said. I said,

—Well, I don't know what I'll be doing this summer, but it sounds good to me. I'd love to go up north.

It was Colin's turn. He had not caught Bitsy's smile. He said,

—Two things: first, I won't be getting a summer job. I have to figure out what to do with my life. There's always graduate school, but I haven't decided about that. Second, it's been my experience that family vacations tend to become family disasters. Why don't we all plan separate vacations, then spend an evening together telling one another about them? That might be less wearing.

There was silence around the breakfast bar. Bitsy and I looked to U.T. He said,

—All right, think about it. It might be fun.

That was it: no blather, no polemics, no theatrics. Colin joined Bitsy and me in staring at U.T. He threw up his hands, but gently.

—I'm not going to coerce or otherwise intimidate you. I think it would be very . . . nice. Just consider it. No need to make plans right now. Who knows, I might have to go to Washington to become the Most Supreme National Poet at the Library of Congress. The best-laid schemes o' mice an' men gang aft agley. The vicissitudes of history make foolish men's plans. We shall see.

—Yes, think about it, Bitsy said.

She was smiling too much and making me nervous.

Something was going on that Colin and I had been left out of. I remembered the huge gaudy flower, but I decided not to bring it up.

Colin looked sick.

—I think I'm going to bed, he said.

It was seven-thirty. Bitsy asked if he wasn't feeling well. She reached across the counter and felt his forehead.

—You don't have a fever.

—I'm just tired.

Colin put his plate in the sink and headed upstairs. Bitsy got up and followed him. U.T. looked at me.

—Do you think you'd like to do that, go up north this summer?

I said it sounded wonderful. We hadn't been fishing in years, I said. We used to go all the time. U.T. then told me about all the other places to go and things to see on the North Shore: smoke-houses where they would smoke fish you had caught; agate hunting on the lake; geological and botanical outings. I said he didn't have to sell me. I would love to go. He nodded, reached out and took my hand. We shook.

—Okay, he said. We'll do it.

—You're on, I said. Right after school lets out.

—Spring will be here in no time.

He looked out the frost-covered window. The temperature had dropped to ten below.

In the living room, after dinner, U.T. and Bitsy discovered the cause of Colin's malaise. I told them about Colin's writing class. Bitsy asked U.T. to go and talk to Colin. U.T. threw up his hands. Bitsy went up herself. U.T. said to me,

—I hope you find something sensible to do with your life.

Bitsy came down and said that Colin was asleep. Then she went to the back closet and brought out the Matisse to show us. We liked it very much. She put it back behind the Hoover.

U.T. and I went to clean up the dinner dishes. He asked me about my day, and I didn't have much to tell him. He asked me about my plans for next year, about college. I told him I had my applications in, mostly to eastern schools, but I didn't know where I wanted to go. He said it was just as well, that plans were conceit and delusion; the best-laid schemes, he said again. He was no longer sure, he said, about the efficacy of will and desire. But it was good, he said, that I had my applications in on time.

As I put the last plate in the dishwasher Bitsy came into the kitchen. She asked if we wanted to go skating. She said a little exercise might be just what we needed. We went upstairs and put on long underwear and sweaters and heavy wool socks. Then we gathered hats, scarves, mittens and parkas and left the house to walk to the skating rink on the other side of the lake.

The night was clear and still, and the stars were out, very bright. It would get cold tonight, U.T. said, with the sky so clear. There was nothing of triumph or glee in his voice. I walked beside Bitsy, who was between me and U.T. The cold was sharp on my cheeks, and I could feel that my lips were beginning to chap. I licked my lips and they stung with the cold. I held my skates one in each hand by the blades; U.T. had tied his skate laces together and hung the skates around his neck; Bitsy held hers under one arm. We walked with the clouds of our breath leading. The trees along the lake were dark, but the air was bright. There was a half moon and all the stars showed clearly. The snow was gray in the dark and white under the streetlights, spaced widely along the boulevard.

We walked past the dark open water, and along the curving shore, where the big island was near the shore. I heard our breathing and saw our breath and heard the creak of our boots on patches of packed snow on the path. U.T. coughed and cleared his throat. Bitsy shifted her skates under her arm. We came in sight of the tennis courts buried in the snow. U.T. said,

—I saw Cy Meyer in the department today. He's back from his sabbatical and a trip around the world. He went to Dublin and followed Leopold Bloom's tracks; they sell annotated maps of it in the bookstores and souvenir shops, he said. And when he was in Paris he went to the *Closerie des Lilas*, where Hemingway used to hang out. There are no Hemingways there anymore, just tourists looking for latter-day Hemingways. And the waiters are not so gracious as they once were, and a beer costs four bucks. He had better luck in Italy—brought back stamps from San Marino, shoes from Rome. And he's absolutely wild for Florence. He couldn't get over the statues in Florence—statues everywhere, most amazing thing he ever saw. And St. Peter's is just like the St. Paul cathedral, he said, only vice versa, since St. Peter's came first and the St. Paul cathedral is only a copy. He liked it, though, he likes them both, in fact. Then he went through Greece and Egypt and Israel, and Tokyo, Hawaii, San Francisco. He wants to come over and show us his slides. Every time he looks at his photograph of the Sphinx, he said, he wants to weep. It makes him think of Yeats, and that makes him want to weep still more: *And what rough beast, its hour come round at last . . .*

U.T. paused. I thought of Molly Bloom, frozen and eternal like the Sphinx worn by wind and sand and time. U.T. said,

—I've never really wanted to go to Europe. I suppose I'd enjoy it. Cy said the Parisians are very unfriendly. He said, and I quote, "They all speak English but they just stare at you with their '*Je ne parle pas anglais*' and make you feel like an idiot."

—My parents took me to Europe once, when I was in high school, Bitsy said. I don't remember much. I remember one time, in England, my parents were just catching on to European accomodations, and they made a point of asking for a room with a bath. Their request was granted, and they felt very world-wise for having figured out these foreigners. And we got to the room and my father went to look at our bathroom, and yes, there was a bath, but there was no toilet. They had been foiled by their euphemisms; the toilet was still down the hall, and they were too embarrassed—too proud, I guess—to complain.

—Your parents travel like big game hunters. They have to bring back trophies or the trip is a waste.

—What about that box of yours in the bedroom closet? Bitsy said.

U.T. did not answer right away.

—That's nothing. Junk, memorabilia. A silent travelogue.

Now we saw the lights of the skating rink. They were yellowish lights set on telephone poles on the shore behind tall piles of snow. The rink was a large oval, about a hundred yards long, plowed clear of snow. Near the shore the ice was bright and yellow under the lights and fell into darkness farther out.

—When we go to the North Shore this summer, I'll find you some nice agates, U.T. said. You can start your own box.

We saw the warming house, a small square plywood building painted brown. Smoke rose from an aluminum pipe on the peaked shingled roof.

There were only a few skaters on the ice. Three teenage boys in sweat pants passed a puck around at one end of the rink. An older couple moved slowly, arm-in-arm, down the dark side of the ice. A younger couple, holding hands, skated unsteadily, swinging their arms to keep balanced. A half dozen more skaters, young and old, came and went from the warming house. It was quiet. The skaters' talk and laughter were damped by the big space and the cold.

We went into the warming house. It was dimly lighted by two bare bulbs in fixtures attached to the beams at either end of the small room. The air was heavy and warm. There was a thick smell from the oil burner, and the smell of coffee warming on a hot plate in one corner, and the smell of cold wool and old wood. The wooden benches were worn, and the nailheads showing on the benches were shiny. The floor was covered with black rubber mats. The ceiling was open to the rafters.

We sat on a bench near the door and put on our skates. No one spoke while we laced and tightened and tied our skates. Bitsy had white figure skates. The toes were scuffed and there was some rust on the blades. U.T. and I had hockey skates. I finished first and went out ahead of Bitsy and U.T.

I slid down the ramp that led from the warming house to the rink. The ice was hard and brittle, and my skates shaved up a spray of ice as I pushed off. I had gone once around the rink when U.T. and Bitsy came out. U.T. steadied Bitsy as they came down the ramp. On the ice they stood for a moment, looking around the rink. I came past them, going fast, and I waved. I turned around and skated backwards to the curve. Bitsy took U.T.'s hand and they started off.

U.T.'s long limbs were even more pronounced when he skated. His long arms swung and his legs kicked out behind him like a wading bird taking flight. Bitsy skated with small strides, pushing with the toes of her skates. She took three strides for each of U.T.'s. U.T. looked enormous on skates. The big red pom on his red stocking cap added three more inches to his height. Bitsy came just to his shoulder.

I came around to pass my parents again, then I slowed and skated with them. Bitsy tugged her scarf up over her nose and pulled her hat down over her ears. She said,

—It's cold.

Her voice was muffled beneath her scarf. U.T. said,

—Tell us about the old days, skating on the prairie creeks in old North Dakota, like Laura Ingalls Wilder.

—We had no creeks, just irrigation ditches. Then they built an indoor rink in the next town over.

—So much for the romance of the prairie frontier.

—There never was much romance. Boredom, wind, and cold. And cabin fever. Life on the old homestead isn't all it's cracked up to be.

—What is? U.T. said.

—That's why my parents live in a museum now.

U.T. looked at me. He said,

—And you, my youngest, how will you remember the care-free days of your youth?

I looked back at him from under the rim of my blue watch cap.

—Fine, I said. It's been just great.

U.T. looked away, ahead down the ice.

—Wait a while, he said.

I skated away, down through the dark and into the lighted strip near the shore. The last skaters had headed for the warming house, and we were alone on the ice. I skated by myself. U.T. and Bitsy skated together, holding hands from time to time.

In less than half an hour I could barely feel my toes inside my skates. My cheeks were numb and my lips were dry and sore. I was ready to go home, and as I came around the curve near the warming house I looked down the ice and saw U.T. and Bitsy. U.T. was skating backwards in front of Bitsy, facing her. He was holding both her hands in his and they moved around the far curve, U.T. pulling and Bitsy gliding, slowly into the light. Then U.T. turned around and pulled Bitsy to him and put his arm around her shoulders and she put her arm around his waist. They coasted gently to the warming house ramp and stopped. I came up behind them and the three of us went up the ramp into the warming house.

There was no one inside but the rink attendant, who watched over things and closed the rink at ten o'clock. He was young and sullen and sat in a corner reading a paperback novel. He glanced up at us as we came in, checked his watch, and went back to reading.

We took our skates off and rubbed our cold toes. The attendant looked at his watch again, then got up to turn the rink lights off. We picked up our skates and left.

As we walked along the path toward home the rink lights went off, one by one—I counted six lights going off—and the path became darker with each light off, and then the path was dark, and the sky became dark again and we looked ahead to the streetlight near the tennis courts. The lights in the houses all around the lake looked bright and warm.

At home we unbundled and sat in the family room to watch the news. We turned on the television just in time for the weather. The weatherman predicted another day of gray cold and wind. He said we might get some snow, maybe a lot, maybe a blizzard, he wasn't sure. Something was happening out west. It would be cold, at least.

The television was acting up. U.T. played with the vertical hold. The anchorman shook his head and the sports was on. U.T. said,

—How long can this cold snap last?

He turned off the television. I heard Colin snoring and mumbling in his sleep. We sat. Bitsy yawned and rubbed her eyes. U.T. said,

—The day is done.

—Time for sleep, Bitsy said.

—Day is desire and night is sleep.

We went to bed.

The third day. Night

ULYSSES TURNER FRASER dreamed that he was in the *Closerie des Lilas*, trying to order an *eau-de-vie*. His students were all around him, dressed as waiters, saying, *"Je ne parle pas anglais, je ne parle pas anglais."* There was a large jade plant on his table. A katydid perched on the jade plant. The katydid said,

—*Tout est pour le mieux. . . .*

Gertrude Stein entered carrying a bottle of violet liquid. She sat at U.T.'s table and poured two apéritif glasses of the liquid. She raised her glass.

—To the triumph of logic, and to that tree whose fruit threw death on else-immortal us, she said.

They drank. The violet liquid tasted like Scotch.

Hemingway came in and took Gertrude away.

—Doctor Fraser has work to do, Hemingway said.

The waiter, whose name was Claude, came for U.T.'s order.

—One true sentence, straight up, U.T. said.

U.T. went to work rewriting his poems, but he kept losing pages. He looked everywhere and couldn't find them. He thought that Claude must have taken them away. Then he saw his students, no longer in waiters' attire, gathered around a table across the room. They were reading his poems and laughing outrageously. U.T. thought what a fine waiter Claude was.

188

He set to rewriting his journal. "I was born in North Dakota, land of clean white churches and Lutheran restraint," he wrote. He did it all over again. He was a poor sod farmer. He hid from the eye of God in a sod-roofed hut. He was happy and humble and he wept for his finite existence and his squalid home.

The *Closerie* was closing down. Claude tossed U.T.'s students, one after the other, out into the street. He came and dropped a heavy white cloth over U.T. and the table where he sat. U.T. remembered that he had an appointment to attend, but he could not remember when or with whom. He noticed that he was already two hours late, then he thought that it had been last week. He couldn't get it straight.

He was on a great desert plain. Molly Bloom, much larger than life, slouched with slow slides of her enormous frozen haunches along the warm earth. She left a trail of matted hair and melt. The earth shook. U.T. was running, calling for Molly Bloom.

The wind was on the wheat.

The sky was dark with thunder.

School bells were ringing.

The day was still dark as U.T. drove to the University. He listened to a weather report on the car radio. With the temperature at twenty-five below and winds gusting to forty miles an hour, the windchill was ridiculous. Exposed skin would freeze in two minutes. A tree had exploded near Lake Calhoun. A big storm was approaching from the West. Blizzard conditions prevailed across South Dakota. The wind before the storm was bringing red clouds of Dakota dust to Minnesota. Red dust already covered the snow and darkened the morning. Schools were closing in anticipation of the storm.

Too late, too late. U.T. was almost at the University. Cars on a West Bank cloverleaf made a circle of light giving on to the Fourth Street tangent, heading for downtown. U.T. remembered circular lights, a ferris wheel, somewhere in Connecticut, at a church fair. In the parking lot behind the stone basilica there were booths and games and a ferris wheel. The basilica turned red, yellow, blue and green as the ferris wheel went around. Catholic children went slowly over the top. On the church lawn a stone Virgin took on the colors of the ferris wheel. The Virgin was red, yellow, blue and green. Down the lawn, in the shadow of the basilica, a stony Christ stood dark.

A small woman dressed in black came across the lawn and knelt on the prayer bench before the Virgin. The woman's face turned red, yellow, blue and green in time with the Virgin. The ferris wheel went round and Catholic children screamed. The woman's lips moved quickly and soundlessly. The Christ stood in darkness. Small Christians ate cotton candy.

The wind shook the car as U.T. crossed the Washington Avenue Bridge. The University buildings were dark. He had left a note for Bitsy: "Getting back on the horse." It was six-fifteen.

He parked in the East Bank Union ramp and walked to the English department. There were papers that needed grading. He would assume his professional obligations. There was something he could do. The triumph of logic is knowing you are useless on this earth. You turn logic on its head; you rejoice in uselessness.

He used his key to enter the English department. The halls were cold. The furnace was on a timer set to come on at eight.

He made a pot of coffee in the department lounge. In his office he drank a cup and smoked a cigarette. Another cup of coffee, two more cigarettes. The jade plant was deserted. In his journal he wrote down the night's dream. He knew it meant nothing.

The papers were from Romantic poetry: "Ode to the West Wind," "Ode to a Nightingale," "Tintern Abbey," "Childe Harold's Pilgrimage."

"The West Wind is the mortality which inflicts us all. The Romantics' main concern was death." A reasonable thought; it earned a "B."

"In our scientific age we no longer look to birds for meaning, however enjoyable their songs." He couldn't agree, but one made allowances; it earned a "B."

"Childe Harold prefigures the modern anti-hero. His quest is for life and to thwart futility." Problems with parallelism, but thoughtful; it earned a "B."

He gave them all their "B" 's with a few random remarks. They would throw them away. It was a neat system, no clutter.

Thoughts of churches, pyramids, and stony-haunched idols troubled U.T. as he read and graded. His college days, all his days, came back to him, like pearls dropping on a string, or like pearls before the swine. Words and things, sights and memories, chaos, finally.

He remembered a trip to Nova Scotia. He had walked and hitch-hiked along the southern shore, then across the peninsula to the Bay of Fundy and south again in a circle to where he had begun. All along the way he saw the low coastal homes and white clapboard churches of fishermen. The churches had low bell towers or spiral-shingled spires that seemed to stop before reaching their expected height, as if the lesson of ambition were a tenet of local architecture. It was low country; the land slid easily to the sea; the people were small and stout, on the whole, like shoreline trees. Two centuries of conflict and many more of hard weather had rounded things down to the point of least resistance, where resistance became feasible.

Then, coming up from Fundy in the poor French section known as Acadia, U.T., accustomed to lowness, silence, and humble architecture, was stopped—not quite by a light from heaven—on the road to Yarmouth, by what he saw. A cathedral stood—not stood, soared—on the flat marshy coast: a white granite Gothic height three times as high as any wooden meeting house on the southern shore. "God is on our side," it said, not a boast, but a fact graven in faith. For a moment U.T. knew faith. There was no sense to it; it was completely insane; it could not be explained. U.T. thought: "These people know joyful noise, laughter and weeping and terrible cries." The vision shimmered in heat off the highway. "It is a mirage." He came closer. "It is real. It is enormous and white. It is made of stone and glass."

Inside it was cool and bright. Blond oak pews reached a great length to the altar, to the suffering gilt Christ in a dark niche on his stanchion. Marble saints filled the niches along the walls. The weight of the stone became illusion under the light through stained glass on white walls and floor. U.T. sat and thought: "It is completely insane."

On a table near the door there were brochures and schedules of events in French and English. There were also color postcards of the cathedral that did it no justice at all. The postcards cost five cents. There was a coffee can for the change, the honor system.

That was something U.T. had seen, that and the Connecticut church carnival. There was the burnt-out church by the Boston overpass, trackside tenements, towns built in strip mines, flaming black oil refineries at night. He had seen all those things. They were things he could think about. To what end? Could you follow the thread through a dirty city or into the desert to the home of a rough desert beast? Could you burn your eyes out looking for its eternal principle? Would you want to do that? In our scientific age our scientific people would laugh at you. They would call you crazy when you charted the pattern of scattering sparrows and announced the news of eternity. You would never do that, though you might wish you could. They would not know what you meant when you told them about a church in Nova Scotia. Or, they would, but you wouldn't.

Where was the katydid? Nowhere in sight. The jade plant was squat and impassive. Just like an insect to desert you in your moment of need. The katydid's comments were mockery. *Tout est pour le mieux*, the katydid said, but he left out the punchline, the little bastard. The world is a dangerous place for poets, and children bring you nothing but worry. The situation was serious, as serious as a carnival.

Where was the katydid with its mocking comfort? *I should have been a katydid, sitting on a jade plant, a squat and jolly jade plant, singing all the day*. The building was empty, but U.T. heard words of ridicule barraging the walls of his office. "Here we go, boys—U.T. Fraser: 'Don't ask me, for I don't know; I know nothing, but everything you don't know, I know.' The sniveling aesthete, dreary dilletante, with his cultural critiques and gratuitous condemnations. And he never pays for coffee, thinks it grows on trees. Thinks we owe him something. Well. . . ."

la-de-da and la-de-da-de, singing all the day

The sun's first rays lit the bridge, the river, and the West Bank buildings. The heat came on early, the timing was a little off. The radiators knocked and sang.

la-de-da-de all the day

U.T. skimmed through the papers and assigned them all

"B" 's. There was no justice. He went to warm his hands by the window radiator.

all the live-long day

✂

Bitsy, Colin and I watched the weather from the kitchen window. The hazy wind moved down the alley; it sucked away snow from the yard in sudden plumes; it sublimed the frost on the windows. "Gale force winds are stripping ton after ton of South Dakota topsoil," the radio said. Already the snow around the house had a reddish tinge, red South Dakota topsoil.

The barometer was falling steadily. When the northern front met the western front there would be a terrific blow. Bitsy called the women who worked at the gallery, and told them not to bother going in.

—Maybe you boys should stay home, she said.

—The University never closes, Colin said. I'll go, my professors will have called in sick, and I'll come home.

My private school was also among the last to close. Will and resistance were what defined the elite, Bitsy said.

—I don't know. It looks terrible out there.

She touched the memo pad with U.T.'s note, "Getting back on the horse." With her fingertips she pushed the pad to the middle of the counter.

Colin and I finished our breakfast and walked to the bus stop. Colin said something to me, but I couldn't hear him for the wind. At the bus stop he tried to light a cigarette but the wind kept blowing his matches out. One of the businessmen gave his lighter to Colin. Colin got the cigarette lit and the wind then blew the ember off. He crushed the cigarette into the reddening snow.

We pulled our scarves over our faces and turned our backs

to the wind. The businessmen looked ludicrous but cheerful in their Burberry coats and colorful stocking caps. We stood in a clump facing east. The clump turned as one at the sound of the approaching bus.

Bitsy remembered North Dakota storms. The prairie wind blew all winter, so that its sound was like silence. There were sometimes drifts up to the eaves. The roads drifted over in no time. Very rarely the southern edge of a hot chinook would tail across the state, melting several feet of snow in a matter of hours.

She had never been frightened by storms. She thought of her birthday just past and the growing fears that age might bring. She thought about her parents, who seemed to have crushed such fears by remaking themselves, renouncing the early sources of unease and conscience. What would life be like without some guilt and regret, some forgotten secrets, without something to keep you honest?

The airport had closed.

No travel was advised.

Grocery stores were being deluged with people stocking up on food. The radio announcers recalled the Great Armistice Day Blizzard of 1940 that killed forty-nine people, and other great blows of the century. This storm was already history. History was less dangerous than weather. No one died in history; everyone there was already dead. If you were alive in history you would stay that way. In some later history you might be, certainly would be, dead, but for now you were safe. You could not become complacent, of course, or history would trample over you, perhaps in the guise of weather.

Bitsy picked up the phone to call U.T., but the line was dead.

She went into the dining room. The swans were not on the lake. There were no ducks, no geese. There was no sign of the

Latvian lady. Bitsy imagined the Latvian lady at her own window, wherever it was, looking out on the weather and worrying for her Swanee. Swanee would be all right, or he wouldn't. Birds did die. Winters like this were hard on the birds, hard on all of God's creatures.

Colin did not bother to confirm that his classes were canceled. He went to the West Bank coffeehouse on the corner of Cedar and Riverside. He thought about Marcos, he thought about distance.

Bearded vegetarians came into the coffeehouse, clapped their hands, stamped their feet, rubbed their red cheeks, and made it known that they were extremely healthy and enjoyed this kind of weather. Colin sat and smoked. He looked through, but did not bother to read, the new crop of slogans and announcements on the windows. He wondered if his novel was right for the times. He wondered whether revolutionaries always had to die. That could be it: all along you know Marcos is going to die, and then he doesn't. He lives to affirm life and a balanced sense of the world. He says, "Wait a minute, let's look at what we've got here: one entirely senseless world in the midst of a senseless universe, and absolutely no reason to live, to keep living, to struggle to live, to suffer under our defective consciousness, to wither under our conviction of mortality, to bring forth more bodies and souls to suffer what we have suffered, to continue to perpetuate a ridiculous, a finally fatal situation—no reason for any of it, no reason for a single thought or action, nor for kindness, justice, humility, charity, sympathy, rationality, love, forgiveness or acceptance. This is what we have, and what shall we do? We shall live! O, praise, we shall live! In the face of inadequacy, confusion, cruelty and chaos, shall we live! Praise!"

Would Marcos say that? Marcos of the fierce beard and the

wild eyes, denizen of the unanimous jungle, retrospective native of the green-tented land? It would take some doing, but the lives of fiction were malleable, to a point. Colin flipped through his pages, where Marcos truly lived. Nothing quite so upbeat as Marcos' imagined monologue, no conversion was possible in this context. But he might live, humbly, somewhat surreptitiously, perhaps, he might live. He would live, might eventually give praise, and that was enough. Colin wanted to tell that to Bates and to his cynical classmates who coveted their own provincial lives. Someone was alive in these pages, someone lived and would live. That is enough, Colin thought, or that is a start. You, Marcos, though the hungry generations tread you down and you mourn the death of the true Ramon, yet shall you live.

The sidewalks of Cedar–Riverside were empty save for a few blond and ruddy denizens in down parkas. Big weather brought out the true character of a neighborhood. Colin realized that he was not an outsider here. A certain sensibility still prevailed in these streets and in the dwindling coffeehouses and the local beer joints. He imagined a nurturing eclecticism— East Bank, West Bank, he could move in both worlds, though the business-minded students would continue to trudge past his window. They might come around, might eventually become good people. Such charitable thoughts surprised Colin. He thought that they would likely pass.

But Marcos would return to walk these streets. The final scene: Marcos appears on a West Bank street corner, his wild eyes a bit sunken, contemplative, the hard twist of his mouth softened, tolerant. And all those who had secretly awaited his return greet him. He would tell what he had seen, and something might be learned. Marcos will have learned; he will have survived the temptations of drugs and sex and Marxism. That rang a little flat. He will have learned and be learning.

But again, there was another Marcos, with eyes not so wild and beard less fierce than those of him who mourned the death of the true Ramon. What if the mundane—that is, the *real*—Marcos returned before the fictional one? That would spoil everything. But there need be no confrontation. The lives of life were as malleable as those of fiction. Marcos is twins, or the names are but coincidence. Coincidence was permissible in life, though not in fiction. Coincidence between fiction and life was sometimes to be expected, though too close a correspondence could be unnerving.

Colin put on his coat and left the coffeehouse. He walked toward the West Bank buildings and the Washington Avenue Bridge. He was going to see U.T., to tell him what he had discovered. Marcos will live and give praise, though quietly.

The halls of my school were all but empty. One other quality of the elite is its ability to resist its own institutions. The parents had kept their children home, school or no school. The weather was unbelievable.

Most of the teachers had stayed home as well. My chemistry teacher had made it, but that class didn't meet until afternoon. I doubted that the administration could hold out that long. I wandered down to the music room. The glee club conductor was there, and we went through my solo a few times. "Lord, if I got my ticket, can I ride?" "Ride away to heaven this mo-horn-in'," sang the conductor, whose voice was nasal and flat. The wind hissed and whooshed and rattled the windows. It was all I could do to hear myself above the noise. The conductor, the wind, the piano and I were all off key. I sucked a piece of lemon to clear my throat. "Hear a big talk, of the judgment day . . ." "Lord, if I got my ticket, can I ride?" We gave it up. I went back to the pub room.

The pub room was colder than usual. A dusty draft sifted

under the windows. Outside, the wind was visible; it was red. On the floor there were six big boxes of newspapers that were supposed to be distributed today. There was no one to read the news, no one to appreciate the fine job we had done of ordering the last week's history and preparing the future. I took one copy, cut off the front page, and taped it on the wall along with those of the previous weeks since September. "Radiators don't work in several rooms," one of the headlines announced. "Contention experts in Nationals?" ran another, with the kicker, "It's debatable, forensics coach says." I had written that one. The quotation was fabricated, but the head-line needed some punch. He might have said something like that. He was always very cautious.

I sat in the armchair and remembered my rememberings. "If this damned rain were snow we'd have a foot," I remem-bered U.T.'s saying. He would have his snow. He would have snow and wind and cold, drifts feet deep and frostbite and all manner of disaster and misfortune, a conquest of weather over civilization. Civilization would sit up and take notice, then forget all about it. U.T. thought that people should appreciate the weather, take account of the physical world. It was impor-tant to think about membranes and sinews, glands and arteries, veins, joints, cartilage, sweat, bile, mucus, bone and muscle. Then, if you had the leisure, you might consider electrons and birdsong. Start from the bottom, but it was hard to do. Even talking about it shifted the emphasis. Storms like this were helpful in getting back to basics. And cold was good, too, for setting things apart. The cold pushed in around small bodies carelessly radiating their vital heat as if trying to warm the universe. Like an infra-red photograph of heat loss, the cold defined the essential. Storms like this announced once again the primacy of the elements, gave credence to outmoded notions. Earth, wind, water and fire, however we may protest, will have their way. Sophistication was another name for delusion.

I looked up. I must have been off somewhere. Calvin, the custodian, was standing in the door, rapping on the jamb.

—School's off, he said. On account of nobody's here. You heard that joke, "What if they held a war and nobody came?" That is our situation.

Calvin had been in the navy; he thought of the school as a ship of which he was captain. Calvin was accustomed to finding me in a bit of a daze in the pub room armchair after hours. We had become something like friends.

—Thanks, Calvin, I said. They put up a good fight, though. They would have gone down with the ship.

—City hall and the weather is two things you can't fight, Calvin said.

He made a backhand poke with his mop at a ball of dust skittering down the hall. He said,

—You going to be here a while?

I said I supposed I would clean up a bit. I gave him a copy of the paper to read after the principal and her adjuncts had left. He made a mock lunge with his mop, winked, and went off down the hall.

I sat back in the chair and listened to the wind.

The sun's first rays had been quickly eclipsed by the clouds. U.T. sat in his gray office. Outside there was a gray sky and red wind. U.T. had often gone to the prairie; now the prairie came to U.T. Hit the dirt, he thought, get down, stay low. That was the purest of instincts. Hold on for dear life.

In the hills of my home country I was farther abroad than I knew, memory tells me. I took no account of the bedrock or the destination of the thousand mountain streams.

The whine of the accordian and the scrape of the fiddle

shattered the golden music box. Open the box, all hell breaks loose. Swing your lady, hard, fast, spin and spin, tighter and tighter, and disappear, immolate, the way of all flesh. *This is the way the world ends.* . . .

Someone knocked at the door, the doorknob turned, the door opened. Caroline came in.

—Hello? she said.

U.T. rose from his chair.

—Caroline, what do you know? Come in, sit.

Caroline pushed back her long hair, tangled by the wind. *Have you noticed how the earth is spinning about? spinning like crazy,* U.T. thought. *Why do we stay here? How can we stand it?*

Caroline took off her parka and draped it on the chair. Her lips were chapped and red, her cheeks red and mottled. She wore a red sweater and a gray wool skirt and tights. She rubbed her hands on her thighs.

—Your legs must be cold, U.T. said. Wind must come right up your skirt.

Caroline opened her mouth to speak, then lowered her eyes and nodded.

—It's cold, she said.

U.T. offered her a cigarette which she refused. U.T. looked at her and noticed that she was young and pretty. Her face was red and mottled; how could he have thought her devious? Caroline reached in her bag and pulled out a notebook. She took some typed pages from the notebook.

—I have some things I'd like you to look at, if you don't mind, she said. Some poems. I'd like to know what you think.

U.T. reached out. Here they were, the adolescent love poems, he had been right all along, she masked her lust in meter. U.T. glanced over one of the pages.

—Oh, don't read them now, I mean . . .

She was on the edge of her chair, her arm reaching out. Her fingers were long and thin. She was quite tall. U.T. set the pages down.

—Sorry, yes . . . I'll look at them.

He tapped his fingers on the pages turned upside-down on the desk. *Take account of your days, Caroline, keep your eyes open, be humble and sharing, hold on for dear life,* he thought. *I could tell them something, I could tell them . . . I would tell them, better that a millstone were hung round my neck and the attribution of guilt is universal.*

—Something else I can do for you?

The red was fading from Caroline's face, her skin was white and smooth. *What do I do now, try to seduce her? What is this about, a withered phallus?*

—Have you read my paper yet? I wrote on "Nightingale."

U.T. riffled his thumb along the stack of papers, each with its "B."

—I'm not sure, no, I guess I'm not quite finished. Monday, I think, I'll have them on Monday.

I should have been a poor sod farmer, a withered phallus, a spotted lung, a pair of ragged claws. I should have been, I am, we are strangers, far abroad. U.T. noticed that Caroline seemed soft and young and brought him love poems, lust masked in meter. He offered her another cigarette and she again refused.

—It's no good, U.T. said. Never mind. Do you know my son, Colin? He's a writer, and not too bad.

—I had a class with him once. I like him.

—I haven't been much good for him, though. He smokes too much, but I think he'll be all right. What are they saying about my little tirade? Are they still talking? But that was only yesterday, wasn't it.

Caroline shifted in her chair, fixed her hands on the edge of the wooden seat.

—Doctor Fraser . . .

—Call me Ulysses. My friends call me U.T.

—I was just in the lounge having a cup of coffee. I had nothing to do with all that. They meant no harm. They didn't know.

—Yes, they take off all the professors. They meant no harm.

I could see from their courtesy that we were strangers. The wind had shifted down to the southwest and was rising to join the northern front. *I should have been a katydid sitting on a jade plant and*

—I respect you very greatly Doctor Fraser.

this is the way the world ends. Caroline was young and pretty. Her sweater outlined her breasts, her thin waist and hips. *I should try to seduce her,* U.T. thought. *She might bear me many children. I have nothing to give her, a sere and noisome hole, a desiccated cunt, I am, a poor wayfaring stranger.*

—They're just kids, trying to be rebellious.

This is the way the la-de-da . . . What am I thinking, change the subject. I am a scrofulous bit of flesh. It is cold. The wind blows some things we know.

—Give up on poetry, Caroline, take to fiction, for it may be true to itself. I was telling my kids the other day—I have two, I'm making this up—I was telling my son Colin, be proud to be writing fiction, for it may be true to itself and reflect the whole of existence. Aim for the truth. You have to make it up. You'll kill yourself writing poetry.

—I'm sorry, I should have stopped them. They were just showing off, they'd never say a word to your face.

—My wife is forty-five years old and her name is Bitsy. It's absurd.

Molly Bloom descends a rough high mountain, tearing her flesh on the stone. It is my fault, the cold.

—Have you ever been to the North Shore, ever walked on

the height of land? I'm going there this summer, my family and I, as soon as it's warm. Spring will be here in no time.

Caroline put on her jacket and wrapped her scarf around her neck.

—There's no hurry about the poems, whenever you have time. I appreciate it.

—Do you remember your jump-rope rhymes and hop-scotch jingles? Do you remember the fairy tales your parents read to you, full of monsters and devils and death and disease? Teasdale is preparing an essay on them. They tried to tell us right from the start. Why should we have cared? We were having too much fun.

—I heard they're going to close the University. I have to go catch a bus. Everything is closing down.

Take account of your days, Caroline, hold on for dear life. I know some things, I know these things are true, they just don't make sense, that is all, they're just crazy, that they should be true, it's completely insane.

—Good-bye, Caroline. You won't be in class?

—They're calling off school.

—I'll look at your poems. I'll have the papers back on Monday, I think.

I saw a church in Nova Scotia. I set a jar in Tennessee. It's all the same, it's all the la-de-da-de-day

—Good-bye.

all the live-long day

❧

Colin walked through the cluster of West Bank classroom buildings toward the bridge. The wind and dust stung his face. Business students hurried toward the bus stop. Their briefcases sailed up at arm's length. Everything was closing down. The wind was turning around to the north.

Out of the corner of his eye Colin kept watch for Marcos. How would he know him among the scarf-faced students? He would be carrying a machete, not quite out of his jungle habits. And he would be singing praise. Very few business students carried machetes, and fewer still sang praise.

Colin came to the wide plaza where the bridge walkway split off to either side of Washington Avenue. The wind spun him around to face south. The wind sent him on a diagonal sprawl to the bridge railing. The river lay in ice, and low; dark water eased around the pilings. The ice reached south between steep limestone banks. The ice ran the river. Somewhere south it yielded, maybe as near as Iowa, certainly before St. Louis. The ice stretched around the wide bend and south.

It was senseless to try to cross. The wind was too much. He should be getting home. U.T. was probably on his way home already. Colin turned and headed back toward Cedar–Riverside.

Bitsy, sitting at the window looking out on the parkway, aware of all things, steeped in sensation, committed herself to change. There was no need of blindness, ragged clothes, a rattling bag of seed. There was no need to stand aside while events passed by, to sit patiently holding one's tongue. The need was to speak and be heard, to measure the passing flow and to accord with it. She had been saved from a house on Cape Cod and quiet evenings drinking wine by the sea. She had a chance, and this was her home territory. A forty-fifth birthday was no time to slack off.

She would start modestly. When her parents returned she would give them back the Matisse and the tickets. She would give up her place at the gallery and put her talents to use. She could teach, she could write; there were any number of things she could do, a competent woman, nobody's fool. She could deal in the world.

Then she would sit us down and tell us to shape up. She would tell Colin to stop moping, U.T. to stop blathering and worrying, me to stop taking myself so seriously and have some fun, get a girlfriend, enjoy my youth while it lasted. Her tenure as the quiet observer, the healer and preserver, had served her well in preparing for these changes.

If only the phone worked, she would begin immediately. She would get U.T. home from work and tell him what she had to tell him. He was probably sitting by his window watching the storm, imagining the enormous forces in the atmosphere writhing and coiling and readying for collision. With his imagination he was probably trembling in his seat, eyes closed, listening to the wind. He would exhaust himself with his huge empathy, as if he were an ion in the center of the storm, on the front line, the point of first impact. He would come from the West to meet the North and swirl off eastward. He would be a mass of charged and senseless particles.

Bitsy went to the kitchen and tried the phone again. There was no dial tone, only a faint crackling. The power was still on, though the lights occasionally flickered and dimmed. The furnace burned constantly and the wind rattled the house. The voices on the radio were grim, then joking, warning, friendly. They smothered the storm in anecdotes. They spoke remembrances of winters past: long ago there was more snow; long ago the cold was outrageous; long ago the weather was something to consider. Now there was nothing to worry about. Now we knew how these things worked; God was no longer behind it. It was cold fronts and warm fronts, high pressure systems and low pressure systems, with their isobars and various charges, moist western clouds meeting chilled Arctic air, swirling about, working it out in a purely natural and comprehensible fashion. It still scared the hell out of you. It was better to think of it as the hand of God. That lent some justification. God created pressure systems and isobars to give us something to think about.

Bitsy put the morning's coffee on to warm. God was loosing his fury on the world in the guise of isobars and pressure systems and her family was out there. She knew we had the sense to take care of ourselves; she also knew that accidents happened. A storm like this did not pass without creating its own memories, without taking some lives. The chances were against any harm coming to us, but it would be just like chance to restate its role in the universe by killing one of us.

The voices on the radio described satellite pictures of the storm. It was big, they said, it was hard to describe, but it was *really* big. It swept from the Oklahoma panhandle up into Canada, and from Montana through Wisconsin. It was starting to swirl and it would swirl so fast it would have an eye, like a hurricane. The eye was moving east-by-northeast. It would be over Minneapolis within an hour. Calm would prevail for about twenty minutes; then we would have a storm.

Colin found refuge in Palmer's. On the television over the bar he watched a certified meteorologist describing the significant features of a color weather radar representation of the storm. It was big, the meteorologist said, it was really big. He hadn't seen such a big storm, such a really, very big storm, for quite some time. The color radar picture showed areas of precipitation and varying intensities in different colors. The weather was orange, yellow, green, blue and red. Minneapolis was currently red. That was about right, Colin thought—the wind and snow were red. He couldn't wait for the orange, yellow, green and blue weather. Perhaps they would all mass together and make black weather, black wind, black snow. Orange snow would be nice.

The regular morning drinkers had been joined by a considerable number of students and others seeking shelter. It was like Saturday night; the jukebox whined, the pool balls clacked and rumbled. Colin ordered an Irish coffee and sat at a table near the pinball machines. He took out his notebook and reread the death of Marcos.

Marcos shouldered his gun and looked down across the woven top of the unanimous jungle. At dawn there was movement on the earth, movement on the floor of the green-tented land, conspiracy in the air. He could not yield to his unease. The shooting that had not yet begun was already in his head. The burn of hot metal was in his flesh. He was ready. He called for his men to follow, and they moved, single-file, like a single-minded serpent down the narrow path toward the village.

Later, as he fell, Marcos wondered how they could not have known that the village was fortified. The shrapnel struck his chest and at first it felt no harder than a handful of pebbles. Then the pain spread out from the ragged red mass of his chest. Then a numbness took him.

As he fell he said, he thought he said, "I am an American!" He thought about his high school friends, his useless friends, and a small happiness came to him. This was death. Finally, this was death. He was filled with fear and exhilaration. He hoped they would remember him well.

That was all wrong. Marcos would know, would not be surprised. If the Army of the Revolution would not have a victory, they would have, at least, an honorable retreat with a lesson, a lesson in mortality, and Marcos would learn.

It might have been fate, or God, or chance, but it was will. Marcos willed himself from a death by bullets and flame. "We were reckless," he told his men later. "We cannot afford to be reckless. All we have are our lives." All we have are our lives and our will, he thought. They will serve us as we choose.

That was more like Marcos, the angular man, wiry and wary. There would be no marching off to death, and no mourning for the true Ramon. Marcos was committed to life, for life. Colin worked out a pun on "committed" to give notice to the harder side of things. Committed to this world and this one life, one could only choose life.

The patrons of the bar were whooping and cheering and jeering the weather as if it were the Super Bowl. The meteorologist swept his arms about, bent forward to the camera, grabbed his head, shook his head, laughed; he couldn't stop laughing. With a black marking pencil he drew a great winding spiral across the entire Midwest; the center was Minneapolis. At the center the storm would hit hardest. He punched Minneapolis three times with his marker. The marker broke. He laughed. The camera switched to the anchorwoman. She chuckled and cast a sidewise glance toward the meteorologist. Her face became serious; the crowd at the bar quieted. This was not so funny as some might think.

Colin imagined that Marcos was even now at large on the West Bank. What an entry that would be: at the height of the storm when not a soul is abroad on the streets Marcos springs through the door of Palmer's with gusting shrouds of snow all around him. Silence. He walks to the bar, like Clint Eastwood. He orders a beer and the place goes wild. Drinks are on the house. They dance on the pool table, the bar, the pinball machines. But which Marcos was that? Colin decided it didn't matter. He wrote: *Life, Marcos thought, I choose life.*

The snow had begun. Small icy flakes rapped against the pub room window. This was the eastern edge, not the real storm. Calvin stopped at the door to tell me it had started snowing and I ought to get home.

When I was very young there was more snow. There were tall drifts in the yard in which Colin and I dug snowy chambers connected by tunnels. We sat in the rooms of our snow mansions and the walls iced over with our breath. We talked and imagined. We said, "What if the snow blows across the mouth of the tunnel, and we are trapped here? How would anyone find us? We would melt snow to drink, but what would we eat? Under the snow there might be some berries and things, but that would not last long. Then what would we do? What if they never found us, and we were trapped here forever, or until the snow melted?" Then, when we had scared ourselves sufficiently, we would crawl, Colin in front, toward the mouth of the tunnel. What if? What if? We would find the tunnel entrance clear and scramble out into the light, clamber to our feet, leap in the air shouting. Hooray! Hooray! U.T. was at the window, laughing and clapping. Hooray! He knew what we had been through, how we had scared ourselves silly, how grand was the light. He called Bitsy to the window. She laughed and clapped and hugged U.T.'s waist.

If school was canceled on a day when U.T. was not teaching, he would bundle me and Colin up and take us on a sled to the woods near the house. He pulled us along the snowy streets, making noises like a horse. Sometimes he piggybacked one of us while the other rode on the sled. He was so big, a giant. He could ride me on his shoulders holding both my ankles with one hand while he pulled the sled with the other. He would start to trot, then break into a run, going so fast that Colin and I were wild with fear and delight. He suddenly stopped and let go the sled. We went careening away down the street, shrieking and laughing; we forgot all about U.T. as we sailed toward a snowbank, and he was there at the last moment, grabbing the rope and pulling us away down the street. We laughed so hard.

The rattling of the windows stopped. I started at the silence. The branches of bare trees stopped their whipping and swaying. A few snowflakes eased down through the calm air. This was the calm, the eye. This column of air would lift away, the sky would fly away. The clouds now overhead were thin and broken, mostly gray with bits of white, and here and there a patch of blue. Scattered shafts of sunlight sifted through, the slatted light we used to call Godlight after Sunday school illustrations of Christ or the prophets in gold and purple landscapes. That was how God looked, the evening's last light through leaden clouds.

This was the calm, the eye. It wouldn't last.

At the edge of the woods a rutted, icy road led away into the oak and elm. When U.T. pulled us off the street and into the woods we ceased our laughing and shouting. This was the quiet place. The tall bare elms walled in quiet. The trees cast long gray shadows on the snow. Wind that came and went through the skein of high branches only added to the quiet. U.T. walked softly, almost tiptoe. Colin sat behind me on the sled, his arms and mittened hands wrapped around my chest, while I held fast to quiet and the slats of the sled. The thump of my heart and the rustling of my hair against my parka hood were parts of the quiet.

About a hundred yards up the trail we came to the spot. We moved slowly and watched the high drifts to our right. U.T. pointed for us, but we knew where to look. Suddenly the pheasant burst, flushed, thumping the air from behind the drift, its wide wings slow at first, pounding, then fast and sailing away in a wide arc over the snow with its shadow sweeping fast behind. "The Emperors of China!" we shouted, and scrambled off the sled and into the drifts, and U.T. ran behind, dipping his big hands into a drift and filling the air with snow. "The Emperors of China!"

"The Emperors of China" was the story U.T. told about pheasants. Long ago there was an Emperor of China who lived in a pointy-topped palace of red stone. The Emperor was very old and had but one son who was then still a boy. The palace grounds were littered with jade ornaments and surrounded by a tall hedge. The hedge held the Emperor's menagerie. Peacocks and hens pecked for seed on the lawn. Tigers moved through stands of bamboo. Pandas sat placid in sculpted trees.

Behind the palace were the Emperor's botanical gardens. He grew orchids of every kind and color, violets and delicate fruit trees, and great climbing roses on tall bowers. In the center was a courtyard and a labyrinth planted in jade shrubs whose fat leaves shone like emeralds in the sun.

The Emperor taught his son the meaning of each animal in the menagerie and all the flowers and trees in the garden.

When the Emperor knew that his death was near his son was yet very young but coming fast to his manhood. The Emperor took his son to the gardens and into the labyrinth, where the son had never been. They walked through the labyrinth along the narrow path bounded by dark glossy walls of jade leaves. The Emperor took the correct path without fail, though there were many ways he might have gone, many ways to become lost in the labyrinth.

In the labyrinth's center was a small yard with a fountain pool and benches of jade. Scattered about the pool and benches was a nye of pheasants, perhaps a dozen, moving about, their heads tall on straight necks where plumage shone red, blue, and gold. On the males' chests the colors ran together in a sparkling sheen. Their long tails swept above the close-trimmed lawn, and at their sides they held their strong wings, not clipped; there was nowhere they would desire to fly.

The Emperor sat on a jade bench and his son stood by his side. They remained that way for perhaps an hour, in silence. Then the Emperor spoke. "They might fly, but they do not, and never shall," the Emperor said.

Again they were silent, for a very long time.

Then the Emperor spoke again. Without looking at his son he said, "This is your legacy: a life of beauty and strength, and contentment in knowledge and right." The boy did not understand. His face was still smooth and unmarked by time. His eyes were soft and innocent. He went away with the riddle, leaving his father at the labyrinth's heart.

When he came to the labyrinth gate the son stopped and turned around. The jade hedge was thick, and shadows filled the path. The boy had come through the labyrinth without straying; he had taken the right path without thought. He was ready to take his father's place in the seat of the Emperor.

There were many times, I am sure, when we saw no pheasants, when the tense moment passed and dissipated in the cold air, but I do not remember them. Every time we came to that spot the pheasant split the air, the quiet, with the drumming of its strong wings and swept away in a dying arc trailing its shadow on the snow. "The Emperors of China!" we shouted every time. "The Emperors of China!"

We often heard the Emperors of China when we were home sick from school. U.T. sometimes canceled his own classes to stay with us. He was a rough nurse, flattering us with brusque orders: keep your slippers on, stay under the covers, drink this juice, sit still while I read you this story. The quantity of attention belied his grudging manner. He took temperatures on the hour, kept the bed covered with books and games, staged dramatic readings and sang the songs we loved best.

U.T. was as sad as we were to see those times pass. It took more than a stomachache to stay home from school now, and the attraction was not so great. We had our various responsibilities, and less time for silliness. The great serious world had impinged upon that other, that other world ruled, and joyfully, by silliness, where father and children had conspired to subvert and reject the years' hard passing. We, the children, conspired naturally and innocently; if we had only known then what we begin to know now.

The calm was above us. I ought to get home, I thought, here is my chance to get home. Secretly, I considered that the coward's way out. I should wait for the storm to stake its claim, then head out into its very teeth. But the calm would not last. I would know enough of the storm even if I left right away. I decided to take my head start.

Calvin was sitting at the far end of the dark hall on an overturned wastebasket, reading the newspaper. I waved and he waved and I imagined he winked.

Outside, the air was calm and cold. The snow all around was covered in the fine red dust. I knocked the top off a drift and the snow beneath was brilliantly white. One gust stung my face and died away. I set out homeward at a fast walk.

Bitsy put on long underwear, a sweatshirt, and her warm-up suit. She sat on the front bench and tied on her bright shoes, tied a scarf across her face. She would run while the calm lasted. She smoothed the tight legs of the blue suit and remembered the tennis racket, stashed in her bedroom closet. She imagined herself running along the lakeside path in her blue suit, carrying the tennis racket in one hand. She thought ahead to what sporting bounty the coming years would bring. Next year a hockey stick, perhaps. She would run with a tennis racket in one hand, a hockey stick in the other. Then a baseball glove, a lacrosse stick, skis, a polo pony; she would cart the whole lot around the lake to the amazement of passers-by. And she would run a rope around her waist to hold the Matisses, Picassos, Monets and Renoirs. They would bounce along the pavement. She would be hung with sculpture, and airline tickets would drop from the skies like propaganda leaflets. She

214

would carry the imposed ideas of her others. She did.

She stepped onto the front stoop. The wind had blown a layer of snow and dust over the sidewalks and street. Traffic was heavy on the boulevard as people hurried home from the shortened day of work. Bitsy crossed the parkway and began to run. She kicked away the thin reddish layer that covered the path, leaving her footprints white on red behind her. There would not be much time; she ran hard. U.T. might be pulling into the driveway right now. They were already calling this the Blizzard of the Century. She was out trying to trick the weather, to spit in the eye of God. Come out from behind your isobars, O Lord, show your face.

The elms along the lake began their stark swaying once again. A low stream of dust and fine snow ran around Bitsy's ankles between the snowbanks lining the path. The calm was passing.

The crowd at Palmer's emptied into the streets as a newcomer brought news of the calm. Everyone had heard about the great still eye from the television, and it was a wonder to see it arrived. In their heavy boots they stomped out the door, beers in hand, to see the calm, as if they had never seen still air before. It was very cold. They returned in a hurry.

Colin did not move from his seat. He had been writing fast and intensely. The storm was in him, or he was feeling the Irish coffee on an empty stomach. He had framed a new outlook: he was writing for his times; these were his times; the others had had theirs; a new voice was needed, the only voice that could tell these times, truly and now. He was writing to kill the old man, to kill all the old men, U.T.'s pantheon, and U.T. He loved his father, but the old must die, clear the field. No poems about picnics, no mourning for Keats, no sympathetic nature or babbling of stones. This was his time and in time there would be room, in the museums, for all. Better, in time, to be a moribund exhibit than a sad curator.

The meteorologist was miming the storm. He talked in a low, tense voice, describing the eye, while his arms, stretched out to the side, made small quickening circles. The circles widened as the eye would pass, his voice grew louder and higher, and the manic meteorologist leaped into the air, swinging his new marking pen. Then he stopped, gathered his composure, and "turned it over" to the anchorwoman. She forced a laugh and read the news. Cars were stranded on the state's southwestern highways; someone had died from exposure; the state patrol was helpless. Everything was closing in the path of the storm.

A local talk show came on after the news. Colin lost interest.

He remembered that he had been on his way to see U.T. He could make it while the calm lasted. But U.T. would have left by now; Colin had heard that all classes had been canceled. He would stay here with Marcos for a while, help him on his way to a new life. Colin went to the bar, ordered a beer and a shot, and returned to his table. There was cause for celebration.

U.T. slumped down small in the desk chair in the gray office. The room stank of cigarettes. A gray film of ash covered the furniture, shelves, and window sills. A poster hung on the wall facing the desk, the announcement of U.T.'s reading. U.T.'s photograph, all contrast, no gray, looked back at him. Below the photograph an italic line: *The fancy cheats so well . . .* Your glib denials betray you once again. *The fancy cannot cheat so well as she is fam'd to do . . .* The shadowless face held a slight mocking smile. U.T., his own face flat and ashen, scanned the photograph for any small resemblance. Black points of eyes stared past his head; the black smile curled indulgently. U.T. turned away toward the window. Black points of eyes, black smile, reflected grayly there.

The edge of the river caught in ice, the riverside path where runners ran, a building, some trees, the street, the bridge, more buildings: the objects outside appeared as if painted on the dirty pane. Everything was squeezed flat and wholly visible. If he broke the window there would be nothing there— black space and chaos. The game would be up. Reality admitted only this gray room, this man, his black and white image on the wall.

There were runners on the path, always runners running by the river. They bounced along as if lifted by the wind or tugged on a string. They ran for health and long life and increased potency. U.T. remembered something a friend had told him, an odd thing. She was a runner, and a mother. She said running marathons was like having babies: if you remembered the pain of the first time you would never do either again. You don't remember the pain; you remember the numbness, and finishing. But U.T. thought: you never commit the same motion twice. Maybe the second twenty-six miles wouldn't hurt, maybe the second drop would be easier. Was it the second? Who was counting.

The runners fled across the pane. A squirrel, a tree, some buildings, pressed flat. The city, illusion, the land here was flat. The land was connected everywhere, from the Badlands and flatlands to the eastern mountains it all ran together, around and around, world without end, spinning. *I lay on the prairie pressed flat to the ground; I felt the earth curve; I felt the start of the slow pull; I cried, the terrible slow pull.*

I saw a church in Nova Scotia, high, it was, and like a cry in air. The pull will tear it down, the terrible slow pull.

The eye lay above the city like the spirit brooding. There were no words left that were not packed with shadows and forlorn echoes. Speech would not move the air. Movement itself was impossible, movement through space or time. The mind was wrapped and silent.

No movement showed on the window. The streets, the path were empty. The points of black eyes and black slow smile.

The heat went off. Doors closed, locks clicked. Slurs seeped through the walls like water and pooled at his feet. *Ulysses Turner Fraser is a disgrace to his profession, a middling poet at best and, most damningly, he is a sere and noisome hole. He might be likened to some vulgar larva scrabbling about in its foul and cloistered cyst. His sense of humor is sophomoric.* U.T. sat forward, raised his feet to the rung of the chair.

He turned around again. The window was gone; the wall, poster, file cabinet appeared. Caroline had been here. She lit his cigarettes. A cigarette had burned away to a long gray ash in the ashtray. She didn't want to be his concubine. He couldn't blame her. He was reviled and despised. There were poems on his desk. The bookshelves were crammed with poems, the file cabinet packed full. Cursed rage for order, maddening complusion for the sense of things. We will shake the bones and see how things will be. Throw them, give a good shake, there, they fly and scatter. Try again, or give it up. The bones will not speak today. The air is full of ions; ruins everything.

U.T. put the poems aside. There was no plan for the day, nothing to do, no one to see. His calendar was covered with ash and scribbles spread arbitrarily over the days. Everyone had gone home anyway. Snow fell through the eye of the fifty-seventh freezing day, lightly, through the frozen day cut free of all pretension. The live and sentient day, the sullen night, they ran together, everything, the things pretending wholeness, only the day was whole, and it contingent—the maker's rage. The maker is mad and not to be trusted.

The jade plant held its green amid grayness. The leaves were live and full as they could be, full to bursting. The jade plant swelled and twisted, a ripe tangle, growing and live, the leaves tumid, dark, and moist, roots pushing from every joint. It took little water and senselessly grew. U.T. lit a cigarette. He reached across the desk and touched the burning ember to a jade leaf. The epidermis blackened and peeled, the inner cells ruptured and sizzled wet on the ember. U.T. dragged on the cigarette to keep it going. He took the leaf easily from its branch and looked at the wet black pock the burning had made. He squeezed the leaf, and water flowed up in the pit. He squeezed until the leaf was a small sack of broken cells.

He took another leaf and squeezed it dry. He picked leaf after leaf and crushed the moisture out of them. The water dripped on to the desk, smearing the notes on the desk calendar, running off the desk and on to his legs. Some of the leaves dropped on the wet desk and tried to take back their moisture. They lay on the desk, shriveled and small like popped balloons. U.T. thought the wet was tears. But jade plants didn't cry. Birches and willows wept; jade plants sat stolid and fecund. The tears were U.T.'s, tears for fecundity, the horrible rise of flesh and degeneration under the slow pull. The gyre widened, then turned inward, ever inward, coiling the rapt and silent mind, nothing into nothing.

this is the way

Were they watching? eyes above the window's silted sill? Were they listening? ears against the thin office walls? They were silent. They did not say, *that U.T. Fraser who does he think he is, telling us it all means nothing, hot air and hermeneutics signifying nothing.*

He knew. Everything they said was true, truer than true, for it all meant nothing. He could tell them nothing they did not know. He was the fool, his words nonsense, he the fool for admitting it. He would flee to a Carmelite rock in the hills, or become, himself, a low rock in the path of a poor sod farmer, he the rock and farmer both. He would toil over rocky crops, brood over stones, and they would grow, or they would not, either way it was nonsense, all that remained or ever was.

The dark wood door faced him, closed. The dark wood door opened on to dead black space and chaos.

I should have been:
—a poor sod farmer
—a speechless stone
—a pair of ragged claws
—a katydid on a jade plant
—a withered phallus
—a spotted lung
—a desiccated cunt
—a father to my children
—a husband to my wife
—a frozen desert beast
—a stony Christ, dark and bloodied
—a good and humble man
—a shameless pretender

I should have taken account. I should have seen it earlier. Colin, Bryce, Elizabeth. How will they know me? What will they think? I can tell them nothing, nothing that will help. I am, we are cleft and groping far abroad. My flesh: my sons; my wife. I can't hold, can't help them. I can say, "The world is a dangerous place. . . ."

I should have been a knight at arms alone and palely . . .

I have tried many times to leave this room. . . .

It was apparent that movement was impossible. All the moves were taken and none could be repeated. No words but shadowed and forlorn. Maybe the second drop, if it was only the second, maybe this next.

The door is dark, outside is black and chaos. Here it is gray, there is no light, the river lies in ice, gives itself to ice. In these high latitudes nothing will grow. The terrible slow pull, pulls it all down. There is no blessing in this rage.

All generation is senseless, and fecundity abomination. *I should have been a Shaker priest, too late, too late, abandon hope all ye blessed as I. Too late.*

He wiped his hands across the slurried calendar words. He rose and moved, if movement was possible, toward the dark door. The river lay in ice. U.T. rose and moved, one step, one step, halfway, and halfway again. He stood at the door and faced his image on the wall. He mirrored the slow black smile. All that was behind him was loss and illusion. *The fancy cheats so well. . . .* He stood, hand on the knob. He took a breath. He moved.

I topped the Mount Curve hill and saw the path I had made the night before through the mansion grounds to the fence on the edge of the hill. Bare winter oaks and elms stood straight on the snowy lot. Sumac and wild raspberry brambles filled the open spots—the drive, the mansion's filled foundation, the broken carriage house floor. One large cedar tree slanted out over the fence and the steep hillside. I thought of digging in under the cedar tree to watch the storm. The lower branches, dotted with grayish berries, sagged to the snow. It would be like one of the old snow mansions, with a view. From there I could see the old-time battle of culture versus nature. What I would really see would be nature versus buildings, some snow-plows after a while, not much more. But it would be something to see the storm assaulting the city, to see the first wave of wind and snow rock the tall buildings, to see the snow like wild rivers careening down the walled streets. I would not see that. I wouldn't see it coming. The snow would begin, lightly, and the wind rise, at first in dying gusts, then stronger and gusting against a steady blow, and the snow would become heavier and begin to blow and before I knew it I wouldn't be able to see my hand in front of my face.

The snow was falling lightly. I passed the vacant lot with a last look. The cedar tree shook with a gust of wind.

The houses on Mount Curve were closed and locked, their windows dark. Last night's feeling of exile passed into a feeling of camaraderie. I imagined the occupants of the big rich houses sitting huddled, awaiting the storm. They weren't sitting hud-dled; they were watching television, or eating lunch, listening to music or reading a book. Things were never how I thought they ought to be. People never picked the epic alternative.

The snow came steadily and harder; the wind was low but constant, gusting, shuddering trees. There was little chance that I would be lost or frozen in the short distance from here to home, but I worked myself up a bit. I thought about home. Colin, Bitsy and U.T. would be there, waiting for me. We would have our family vacation sooner than U.T. had thought. We would play games, or sit by the fire, the four of us, reading, or stand at the window and watch the snow. We would listen to the radio for a play-by-play of the storm, and we would gasp and laugh and repeat the storm's statistics in disbelief. It would be another day or two before the city was plowed out—a brief vacation to help us through February and into spring.

The storm was winding up and setting in. I was going down to the lake, down the gradual side of the hill. I saw the trees on the lake's near side; the far shore was gone behind snow.

The bar emptied out with the calm. The morning's patrons left uttering regrets, reluctant to lose the holiday feeling of a weekday morning at Palmer's.

As the crowd thinned Colin began to feel conspicuous and awkward, writing so fervently at his corner table. He closed his notebook and sipped the last of his beer.

When he was writing he had had a feeling that all would be well; Marcos had turned it around, and so, perhaps, had he. When he closed the notebook, the doubts returned. How do you know? How does one ever know? He thought back on the last few days—Bitsy's birthday, the reading, the debacle in class. U.T. had said, "The hard way is to correct as you go, take nothing for granted, act with consummate humility." There lay happiness, or that small satisfaction that the waking man would take as happiness. Then, looking back, there would be something there. But how could you guarantee the past when it was nothing but the product of the present, or of the future, from the perspective of the past? Nothing was fixed, nothing fast, and the facts were never good enough.

Bitsy's birthday: she had been treated badly, taken for granted—the plight of mothers. There was more to it than that, he knew, but that was what mattered now. The reading: the offenses against good taste and the name of literature were numerous, but there was no harm done, really. The naive and the miserable need not be applauded, but neither need they be condemned. And U.T. could be granted his gesture; he had little else. The debacle in class: it was only words on a page, nothing like Colin's true self that had been denounced by his classmates. If they were blind and petty, so they were, and if not, time would tell. Hardly anything was worth getting drunk before dinner and spending the evening with a hangover.

Those were the facts, and they meant nothing, justified nothing. One could not, in any honesty, appeal to the facts for justice, no more than one could appeal to history. It finally came to Colin that we made it all up, fabricated reality blithely and thoughtlessly. That was what U.T. meant. Bitsy's birthday dinner could be remade with one kind gesture, one loving word. The agreement of minds composed reality. Meaning was made, not found. Bitterness and discontent prevailed only if one rejected the necessary making.

It all sounded so nice. For the time it would do, but in time it would become evident that not everyone agreed. The world clung to its facts and anything fast. The warring fictions needed some common ground, call it tolerance, humility, morality—those things we call notoriously subjective. Subjectivity was notoriously meaningless and unassailably true. You took a stand, somewhere, you didn't know. You hoped, maybe you prayed, you kept your eyes open and kept trying. You stayed on guard for the necessary.

Colin, keeper of solitude, walker-alone, got up and headed home. He wanted company. He had things to tell. Marcos would live, and reality was what we made it. Maybe it could not be explained. He remembered one of U.T.'s aphorisms: "Poetry is the clearest, the truest of all language, for it recognizes that words are not things, that explanation is sophistry, and that paradox holds truth." In light of the ultimate absence of truth, one made allowances.

The streets were busy with the last West Bank refugees heading home before the storm. Colin joined a group of University students at the Cedar Avenue overpass above Washington Avenue. The sky was still light gray and the air still calm. Much of the light was lost in the red-dusted snow. The day was still destined for weather.

A bus came up the ramp off Washington Avenue. Colin climbed on and found a seat near the back. As the bus pulled away Colin looked out the back window toward the bridge and the East Bank. At the far end of the bridge Colin saw a figure moving slowly, a man alone on the bridge on the brink of the storm. Colin turned back and rubbed his cold face. He was glad to be going home.

The bridge and river passed from sight as the bus moved toward downtown.

Bitsy almost knocked me down as I turned on to the front walk. She was running hard with her head down. We grabbed each other to keep from falling.

—Mother, I said.

—Bryce! Where did you come from?

Her head was bare and matted with snow that melted and ran down her hot face. We walked to the house, arms over each other's shoulders. The house was dark. Bitsy tried the door.

—No one's home, she said. Where are your father and brother?

I got out my key and let us in. Bitsy kicked off her shoes and went to the phone. She left a trail of melting snow behind her.

—It's working. It was out all morning.

She dialed the English department. There was no answer. The University was all closed up. We sat at the breakfast bar, watching the phone. I put water on for tea.

A few minutes later Colin came in, all smiles. He hugged Bitsy with one arm where she sat, and kissed her on the cheek.

—I spent the morning in Palmer's, working on my novel,

he said. There was quite a crowd, but they all went home when the storm let up.

He sat and puffed from cold and rubbed his ears. A few moments later he looked around the kitchen. He looked around again.

—Where's Dad?

I shrugged. Bitsy shook her head.

The storm had arrived in earnest. It was earning its early praise. From the dining room window we could barely see the trees along the boulevard. The snow came in small grainy flakes pushed horizontal by the wind. The red dust that had come from the west was covered over in a few minutes. Traffic on the boulevard thinned, then ceased. Those who were in were in while it lasted, and those who were out, God help them. The temperature had climbed slowly through the day, and now it was falling. It was down now to ten below.

We sat, the three of us, silent, at the breakfast bar, watching the phone. Occasionally one of us ventured a hypothesis: "He is at the office, but the department switchboard is off"; "He got caught up in his work and didn't make it out in time, but he made it to Palmer's and is waiting it out there"; "The car broke down, but he knows what to do, and he'll be home as soon as a tow truck gets through."

The radio recited snow depths, wind speeds, and temperatures in the path of the storm. Towns in the west of the state had more than a foot of snow with forty-mile-an-hour winds and temperatures of twenty below. There were stockmen's advisories and wind erosion warnings out for the western plains.

Bitsy called the operator to be sure the phone was working. We sat by the phone and waited.

One by one, we left the kitchen. Bitsy sat at the dining

room window; Colin and I sat in the living room. It was still only mid-afternoon, but the light was murky and thin. Colin and I read by a lamp. Bitsy sat in the gray light from the window. There was nothing to see but the shifting outlines of the trees, dark through the snow, and the large dark form of the open water where no swans swam. Snow covered the sidewalks and street. A stream of snow ran low through the street, channeled by snowbanks. The lights of neighboring houses showed dim through the snow. The wind was constant and distracting, depriving us of expectant silence.

We sat, distracted, trying to concentrate on anything but the phone's not ringing, the door's not opening. Night winnowed down from above the snow.

Snow fell and piled, blew and drifted. As the snow deepened the wind eased. Silence came slowly with the deepening snow. The wind kicked up now and again.

By the early evening of turbid light two feet of snow had fallen. In a sheltered spot between our house and the neighbor's, fantastic drifts had blown up. The wind entered between the houses, eddied, and died on the fence across the back. A series of drifts grew up like the sea frozen falling. The halting wind curled the edges of the drifts, shaped the snow over in lovely sharp crests. Where the wave would break and tumble from its height the snow held fast. The tight crest curls opened and widened from one end like cornucopias. From the slope of each drift another rose up. The light from the kitchen window set slight shadows in the troughs. The drifts were staggered and placed according to the wind's angle of entry, utterly random and utterly beautiful. The kitchen light played out to the point where the drifts ended and the wind coursed unhindered.

I sat in the kitchen and watched the drifts. Bitsy still sat at the dark dining room window. I heard Colin moving about upstairs.

Bitsy came into the kitchen and stopped behind me. She stood, silent, and looked out on the small sea of drifts. She put her hand on my shoulder and we watched as the drifts changed shape, slowly, almost imperceptibly, as the wind took snow away here, drew some over the top there, ran through and sharpened the cresting curls, blew away a small drift in making a larger one.

Colin came quietly down the stairs and in to where I sat and Bitsy stood, her hand on my shoulder. He stood behind Bitsy. He put his arm across her shoulders. We watched the drifts in silence.

At about seven o'clock we had a dinner of soup and sandwiches. The snow was still falling. The drifts outside the window went about their quiet changing. As I had watched them they had seemed beautiful; now, as they kept their constant shifting behind my back, they seemed grotesque. They worked ceaselessly and senselessly at their shaping, and all I could do was watch. The wind that moved them had neither sense nor restraint, it had nothing whatever to do with me. Bitsy, Colin and I were caught here watching snow while the world we loved might well have been falling down. Better that the intricate waves all blew away in a sudden gust and left us to our blankness.

We were all, as they say, worried sick. The air was filled not with tension but with impotence, and dread. We could have, should have called the police, the fire department, the president of the University, a lawyer, anyone. We should have gone screaming through the streets crying the fallacies of our blithe assumptions. Hold the show! Stop the presses! we should have yelled. We should have given notice, but we were mute.

We would not take the chance of admitting disturbance in our small universe. In the worst of possible worlds no one could be at fault; the attribution of guilt would be a farce.

As it turned out, the police called us.

⚓

Ulysses Turner Fraser opens his office door and is amazed to discover that space continues beyond the door in an ordinary fashion, into the hall and down the stairs. He walks into the hall and down the stairs.

He leaves the building and enters calm cold air. The students have fled the campus, the mall is deserted, white and flat to the wide stone steps below the Northrop Hall colonnade. The colonnade façade is flat and tall, rising to the peaked pediment. The buildings box U.T. in. He flees down the mall toward the bridge. The calm will not last much longer.

Space continues, spreading, profligate. To the west it sucks around the city and hurtles back to the plains, its source. U.T. is again amazed: the world is so big. He takes one step at a time, puts his feet down solidly: he is moving: one step, one step. The succession of steps is myriad but finite, bounded by mortality. U.T. wonders how many steps he has taken in his life. A couple of hundred every morning before breakfast, probably. His mind falters.

There is the bridge: it channels space over the river. There is the river: it leads space north and south. Its tributaries take space across the continent. The river is the clearing-house of space. The bridge is over the river, high.

This is a day. How many days have there been? That is one he could figure out, the leap years would be a bit tricky, but what difference could it make? He neglects the days and commemoration. It is all a day, one day, one swift circular passage.

The sidewalk widens and gives on to the bridge. The plaza splits to either side of Washington Avenue, on either side of the river, East Bank, West Bank. The enclosed walk-way funnels grayly to the west. U.T. walks outside, on the south side of the enclosure.

Above, the light patches and flecks of blue close over with gray. The clouds begin to course and swirl, it is cold. No place is so cold as that bridge in winter, with the wind down the river.

Buildings, trees, and streetlights exist in space on the West Bank. A bus pulls up the Cedar Avenue ramp and lets on a cluster of students heading home.

U.T. runs his hand along the ice-crusted railing as he walks, step by step, to the middle of the bridge. On top of the steep banks the snow is dusted red, but the red does not reach the river. The color dissipates a few feet down the slope. The river ice is white near the shore, then gray, the bed of gray ice.

U.T. stops, as he often does, at the center of the bridge, to watch the river. Behind him, to the north, the lock and dam sends dark water down to be closed up in ice. There will be no river traffic till the river ices off. Before him, the ice stretches south, around the wide bend. The southern run of ice pulls U.T.'s eyes around the wide bend and south. The river drags south and drops cities on its way: Red Wing, Winona, Dubuque, Hannibal, St. Louis, Cairo, Memphis, Vicksburg, Natchez, Baton Rouge, New Orleans. Then the Gulf reaches out, joins to ocean, surrounds all the land in the world.

Minnesota was once under water, when glacial Lake Agassiz held sway in the North. The lake ran away down the Mississippi via the Minnesota, more moving water than you could imagine. U.T. saw the tides of Fundy, once, taking the ocean out in whitecaps, but even that could not compare. The Mississippi now runs slow and wide in the path of the great glacial river. It runs now under ice along the ancient path, staying low, going lower. The high limestone banks were once brimful and more.

The wind is coming up and the light running away down the course of the river. Snow strikes U.T.'s cheeks. The eye passes, the column of calm closes up, the storm sucks in. The storm has nothing to do with space, it merely fills. Space is there without the storm, surrounding everything, palpable. Space makes U.T. small, holds him close and compact. Otherwise his molecules would disperse and leave him very thin. Space lets him see and be seen, and time makes it unbearable.

Space will let him fall, like every drop of water from the Appalachians to the Rockies, down to the Father of Waters, south and out to sea.

The source of the Mississippi is held to be Lake Itasca, in northern Minnesota. Itasca is a vulgarization of the Latin *veritas caput*, "true head." There are streams which feed Itasca and lie higher than the lake, so the *veritas caput* is in fact a fiction. There are many streams which might be the true head, but they lose themselves in labyrinthine marshes, so there is a commemorative marker where the river empties out of Lake Itasca. U.T. has been there and stepped across the clear stream that becomes muddied, becoming river, farther south. The marker is carved in a brown painted log. It reads:

HERE
1475 FT.
ABOVE
THE OCEAN
THE MIGHTY
MISSISSIPPI
BEGINS
TO FLOW
ON ITS
WINDING WAY
2552 MILES
TO THE
GULF
OF MEXICO

U.T. keeps, in his souvenir box, a pamphlet from the state park at Itasca. "The Upper Mississippi begins in a modest way and flows for some distance in a small and shallow valley. Watershed drainage near the head is imperfect. Many lakes dot the region."

U.T. remembers something else: Lake Itasca is the source of all light, and the air of the earth issues from it in niggardly puffs that grow to encompass all objects caught in space. Space comes from the prairies. Everything is connected, fits together click-snap, so U.T. should not fear to enter the air or encounter the winter waters. It is all created and one. It is very sad.

It is time. The wind is full. It stings U.T.'s face, his eyes, he cries: *The pull.* The river is a swath of white and gray held firm between dissolving banks. Up is down and down is up; the river is an unattainable height.

U.T. remembers: last summer three city boys jumped from the bridge, and lived, as surely they had hoped but not entirely expected. They bobbed up from the dirty sunless depths to praise the light. When they reached the shore all they could talk about was the stink of that dirty river.

U.T. will not surface. He will stay down and head south, take it on the lam for the warm south. When he reaches New Orleans he will climb up the muddy delta banks, through the sodden river flats, and find a place for his new life. He has tried East, West and North; he will try South. He will swagger through the street telling his tale to anyone who will listen; he will make them listen. He will have something to tell them. He will ignore the blow of winter that reaches all the way to the Gulf.

Wind and snow sting his eyes. No place is so cold as that bridge in winter, with the wind down the river. U.T. thinks that the air is really still, but the earth has begun to spin that much faster. He holds tight to the railing. He feels the pull.

The world is a watershed of souls. It's a wonder we can see or think at all, the way time is going by and knocking us around, the way everything is falling down.

U.T. holds fast to the railing. The bridge is his confidant. He has a choice. He could skitter over the railing and shinny down to where the concrete arches support the street and upper walkway. He could arch his back and dissolve into the concrete. But that is a mere delaying tactic, what with everything falling down. He would find the river in time. All the world was biding time, killing time, falling in space.

This is the second drop, this is becoming light again. The snow assures him that flight is possible. The wind is calling out for St. Louis, Memphis, and points south. The Missouri comes in at St. Louis, the Ohio comes in at Cairo. Together they form the great central basin that drains most of the continent. Three great river systems have their source in Minnesota. The northing Red drains to Lake Winnipeg and spreads to Hudson Bay. The St. Louis River skirts the southern edge of the Superior height of land and gives to Superior, through the Great Lakes and the St. Lawrence to the Atlantic. Then there is the Mississippi. It is all created and one, and U.T. wishes he could travel all three. He is impressed by the grand design. But it is all geology and meaningless. The stones never spoke and the stones have no shame. The stones merely abide and erode.

The earth spins around to the final moment like an enormous wheel of chance. Are they watching? peeking out through the plexiglass panes of the walkway? Are they listening? as U.T. cries: *the pull!* Are they choking with laughter, ready to jump out and tell U.T. it's all been a gag? What do they know.

U.T. thinks: Minnesota, Land of Muddy Waters; Minnehaha, Laughing Water; Mississippi, M-I-S-S-I-S-S-I-P-P-I, Father of Waters. We are creatures of water, going to ice. The wind sucks U.T. dry like a flattened jade leaf. He will go to where his vital water lies spent.

He climbs to the railing, feels the terrible slow pull. The world was not made to stage trivial gestures. He wonders if the spinning earth will slap him to the banks before he reaches the river. He must overcome the primary inertia. He looks around, crouched on the railing like a cat. He crouches hunched over the water like the spirit brooding. He sees things and knows their names. He sees the sky. Molly Bloom is out there in smoke and ashes, the cold.

From where he crouches gripping the railing, U.T. surveys the world in a long good-bye. It's all there, no artifice, just the way he sees it. Hermes Trismegistus saw the mundane realm as "a Darkness borne downward . . ., appalling and hateful, tortuously coiled, resembling a serpent." Augustine saw ranks of angels, the fast and the fallen, defining light and darkness. U.T. sees buildings and trees, dark water around the pilings, the riverbanks topped in red, the gray river ice running south. He sees his bare hands, scaly and red, clutching the railing. His hands and face are badly frostbitten. He can no longer feel them. His ears are frozen through. He sees himself crouched on the railing, and that is more than he can stand. He thinks that Bitsy would have a laugh if she saw him like this. He feels the pull, the terrible pull that keeps us here and tears us down. He thinks about his flesh, his sons. He is sorry. In his life he knew love, but like all pretenders he was not content, he squandered, fouled the grain with the chaff. He will take to the air like a bit of chaff and he will land where he may.

Fear death by water. The water waits beneath the ice to take U.T. south.

He lets go, and without even pushing off or trying at all, he drops. Gravity.

He counts:

One-Mississippi, two . . . As he falls the world he knew is wholly transfigured, and he feels that he is seeing for the first time. He gives names: gray-high-above; white-quick-in-space; red-on-the-hill; dark-near-fast. It is a wonderful feeling and he wishes he could go back and try it again with his new-found sight. He feels like the head of a family—he is doing everything right and he knows just where he is going. He is accelerating at the prescribed rate of thirty-two feet per second. He hastens the wind as he falls. The windchill is ridiculous. No place is so cold as that bridge in winter, with the wind down the river.

Two-Mississippi, three . . . He recounts his life one last time: he was a poor sod farmer and the stone in the path of the plow; he was a good and humble man who genuflected before his God. Genuflected! My God! He flattened himself under the very glance of God! He trembled at the sight of Creation. He caressed the earth and lay with stones. How humble he was, and how good, and how mad. He simply could not live. A man cannot live, all flat like that.

Three-Mississippi, four . . . U.T. sees that his naming is nonsense. He gives it up and tells himself his life. He was a poor sod farmer, and low.

There is the river, falling less than a foot per mile on its way to the Gulf.

There is U.T., falling much faster.

There are the banks, going by in brown, black, and white.

There is the river, and ice.

There is my father, gone to water.

In the dark the drifts continued their curling, grainy flow. With the kitchen light out relief vanished, intricacy dissolved to gray and flat. I could pay attention to nothing; there was nothing fast; the necessary fled with sight.

The sidewalk, street, trees, lake, all markers of depth, all gone. The wind pulled snow across the open flat, leaving snow, taking snow away. The snow deepened, settled, covered: grass, pavement, leaves, bushes, weeds, roses, ice, the lake, roofs and doorsteps. The furnace wheezed, we sighed and settled, then shifted, twitched, fretted.

In the dark the snow continued. It covered everything, it blew and drifted, usurping, strangely darkening. We sat frightened, fearing.

I stood in the dark kitchen looking out to the dining room. Bitsy sat at the window. The foyer light lay a yellow square across the dining room table. Bitsy sat beyond the light. The scene was still as if painted, framed by the kitchen doorway. Bitsy was small in the middle ground between the half-bright table and the wide opening of the window to gray light. Then I was not watching through the door. I was part of the scene; I was the morbid patch of light on the dark wood table; I was light clinging tight to the dark damping wood. I was aware of each of the frame's infinite points, more than aware, I was each point. I was infinite by virtue of being light. I settled and dissolved in my all-knowing, all-being.

I knew something was wrong. Someone was in trouble, out in the snow. Bitsy rose from her chair and I could not see. Then I saw her coming toward me, through the door and into the kitchen. She turned on the light. The light was on, the kitchen bright. Bitsy moved toward the telephone. She reached out her hand, and the telephone rang.

She stopped, her hand shaped for grasping, a few inches from the phone. The phone rang, loud, like a scream. Bitsy's hand relaxed. She lowered her hand slowly toward the phone. She picked it up. She listened.

The man—he was a captain or sergeant or commander of some police department—said they had fished U.T.'s body out near South St. Paul where the warm stockyard flow stemmed the ice. Someone saw him jump. It was quite strange: he had been crouched on the railing and someone in a building, seven stories up, on the West Bank, had seen him crouching there, and had run down and out toward the bridge, but it was too late. The witness saw him down on the river, sliding through a split in the ice, then down, away, south. The police had gone and waited near the stockyards, where mist rose thick off the warm bloodied waters. That was their only chance; they hoped he hadn't gotten snagged along the way. It took several hours, but he made it through, and they pulled him out.

Whether he was aiming at the water around the pilings of the bridge, they did not know, but he had hit the ice and crashed right through. He was quite a big man. How much did he weigh? The river ice was the thickest in years. But then, in a fall from that height, his momentum would have been considerable.

An accidental epitaph: "Ulysses Turner Fraser: His momentum was considerable." By the simple virtue of his physical properties and the gross ways of the world U.T. had made it through the ice and south, a ways, to the stockyard dumping pond.

Someone would have to identify the body. That would be impossible tonight, with the snow, and the car was still at the University. There was no hurry, they were sure it was him. The man read U.T.'s driver's license to Bitsy: six foot two, one hundred ninety-five pounds (yes, there it was, a big man), green eyes, red hair (it looked more brown, but it was wet and muddy). It was very strange. They were very sorry. They would have come in person, but the snow. The snow would be ending, and temperatures rising, tomorrow.

Bitsy nodded her head. She made a small thin noise, then put down the phone. She sighed and relaxed, as if a worrisome appointment had been canceled. I felt a strain in my wrists and noticed that my hands were gripping the counter's edge. I turned my head quickly around—I don't think I heard anything—and through the door that led to the back hall and foyer I saw the railing below the stairs' middle landing, and Colin's hand on the railing. I turned back and looked at Bitsy. She massaged her temples tensely. I looked into the dining room. The window was black from where I stood in the kitchen light. Colin came down the stairs. He stood in the doorframe across the narrow back hall. His face no longer looked fat, but drawn and tense. He looked at us as if he had just discovered some terrible secret we had been keeping from him, and did not know whether to accuse us with the terror or the deceit.

I do not know how long we remained like that, the three of us standing, spread and alone, silent. We knew the worst because anything but the worst would have called for words. In our silence we needed words, but nothing else did.

Bitsy had to say something, she knew. I don't remember what she said. It didn't matter. She might have said,

—His momentum was considerable.
and it would have sufficed. She might have said,

—The river ice is the thickest in years.

She told us what she had heard, somehow. Then we stood in the kitchen, not seeing one another, thinking about what we had heard. We stayed that way for a while.

Then I looked at Colin. He was crying, his hands over his face. He turned away and went up the stairs. He had so recently been so happy for the first time in such a long time, and his world was now gone to ruin.

That moment was the triumph of logic, the snap in the limits of reason. Our thoughts fled back, frantic, through the days and events, seeking cause, and of course, there was none. It was just the world, how the world happened to be. U.T. would have been as bewildered as any of us, probably was, even as he crouched on the railing and saw, sadly and finally, his destination. But how we wanted cause, more than we wanted U.T. back, then, because U.T. wasn't coming back and wanting that would be fatal, but we held to cause as something real and true, something God-given, our one small clue to the world. Our assumptions, our most precious fictions, turned sour, and we mourned for their loss as much as for the death of U.T. Or, we mourned one thing only.

I sat in the living room and tried, out of modesty, not to hear Colin's sobs from his bedroom upstairs.

I sat in the chair where the last evening I had watched Colin, drunk. Bitsy sat in Colin's place, her legs pulled up beneath her; she cried quietly. She clenched and unclenched her fists slowly and rhythmically, digging her short nails into her palms. I watched her hands, just for something to watch, to fill the blank. I was not crying, not thinking, or hardly thinking. I took one small thought from watching Bitsy's hands.

Colin's crying grew quieter. Bitsy's hands kept up their clenching rhythm.

It was worse because U.T. was out there, dead, somewhere, we did not know precisely where, and we were here, snowbound and silent. He had always come home, we all had always come home, though any one of us might not have come home on any one of myriad occasions. If we sat clench-fisted every time one of us ventured into the world we would have clawed our palms raw, and perhaps we should have. We should have gone through our lives with nails in our palms, martyrs to senselessness, as if that would redeem anything. We couldn't do that, couldn't even think it. We substitute a little of the parents' insomnia, waiting to hear the car in the driveway. And we try to give in to sorrow, sometimes, though we do not know its true source, or its meaning, because resisting it was to die in the senses.

I looked from Bitsy's hands to her face. The skin below her eyes was dark and damp. Her eyes were closed tight. Tonight blindness would be a virtue, because the world had become so hard, the familiar was mocking and horror. It was all in the head: the world endured, mindless, as ever. But the snow outside *was* horror, the snow fell, covered, fell, and deepened. The snow was horror when it should have been beautiful. The world merely is, and we are multiple and suspect. We were horror, branching arms of dread, capped with a head of despair. But for our sorrow, we would have vanished.

I began to cry, suddenly, from hot dry eyes. I was not light and infinite. I was sorrow and small. I thought: *My father is dead.* I echoed the word a thousand times in my head, and it lost nothing by repetition. In the game of redundancy, death won out. Ubiquity was death's forte, where life and happiness withered under emphasis.

People were always leaving our house. We had to stay there, think death and mourn. Now blindness would serve to hold our sorrow this side of sanity. We would watch the nails in our palms, or feel their sting and the sick swelling in our chests, the hot behind our eyes. Or we could go the way of U.T., fling ourselves into the storm and dissipate in an entropic flush.

I thought about the pheasants, the Emperors of China. I did not see the bird spring flushed from the drift, but only its fast shadow on the snow. I imagined that when the pheasant settled in some safe thicket the shadow fled on, witless and swift, a bird-shaped darkness, fleeing. The shadow was edged in penumbra, neither light nor dark, a mongrel shade of particles and waves. The shadow makes things full and lets us see.

I remembered a night on Lake Superior, one night of U.T.'s birthday sailing trip. We were anchored off one of the Apostle Islands, and the night was clear. The moon was less than half full, and waning, but the lake was still and the night bright with reflection. The light on the water tricked out the path of any slight breeze and the ripple arc from the boat. I looked at the moon, nothing grand in its shape, and I saw not only the illumined crescent, but the darkened part, as well, the larger gray that joined the light. I saw the curve of the moon, its enormous globe. I wanted to reach out and bind myself to the great joining curve, hold the moon in my arms and legs, and spin, around and around, lighted and full, wherever the galaxy might wander. I watched the moon until it began to descend and lose its shadow, or until I got tired and went to bed. The next day was the day of fog and calm, shadow all around. We were stilled on a flat gray sea.

We heard the whine of a coming gust before the rattle of the windows. We heard blown snow sifting against the panes. Bitsy opened her eyes and wiped them with the back of her hand. She looked toward the windows that gave to an unfamiliar terrain of whiteness and flat. She looked at her red palms. She rubbed them together. She crossed her arms. She shivered.

I tried to sort things out; I tried to think what I was feeling. My father was dead. My father had killed himself. Why did he do it? That was to say: what did it mean? It had to mean something. It had to mean everything, or nothing. But that was not the question. What mattered was making simple sense. That would take time. For now my dead father was a bamboo grove, a frozen cat, or a room full of balloons; he was a galaxy, a snowstorm, a clutch of ring-necked pheasants.

And we were a family now, we three. We three, maddened and mourning. I had always heard it said that mourning was not for the dead, but for the living, since the dead could not care less. I thought of U.T., crouched on the railing of the bridge, frostbit and lost, and I could not believe that was true. It was true that U.T., dead, could not care less, or more, or at all. But once he had cared, and deeply, and for that we grieved. I thought we grieved for the dead. To mourn for the living was the deadliest kind of nihilism.

I thought of Colin, upstairs, broken and spent. Maybe for him it was different, the eldest son. He was almost Ulysses Turner Fraser. That was the shape of Colin, almost his father. But Colin would not ascend to the seat of the Emperor simply by virtue of being male and older than I. Primogeniture was passé. Bitsy was here, and if I sometimes idealized her, I nonetheless knew her hard spirit, her quiet power that had nothing to do with passivity. Under U.T.'s tutelage we sometimes let ourselves be carried away by mythical thoughts and eternal designs. Bitsy always had been, and now very clearly was the center of our family, the one who could live with nails in her palms. We had a kind of trinity left, but no one fit his role. It was just as well. There was no virtue in being immaculate. We were all sometimes helpless, sometimes strong, always bloodied and soiled. The seat of the Emperor was up for grabs. Who wanted it? We all solved the labyrinth every day. Maybe that was what U.T. meant. Dazzled and terrified by the walls of jade, once and finally, he lost his string. If he hadn't been gored he would have wandered into madness and death. The prairie was a labyrinth, and the mountains, the wind, snow, river, sea. Who knows? I tried to sort things out. The philosopher stands in darkness in the mouth of his cave, looks around, furtively, scurries out, shouts something, then runs back inside. What kind of way was that to live? Better to take your truths from bamboo groves, ring-necked pheasants, katydids. At least the fallacy was ingenuous. After all the talk and guesses we arise, stretch, rub our eyes. We pause, we sigh, we shrug. We raise our hands in humble supplication. We go to bed. That is one level of understanding, the triumph of logic, and its refutation. If I find out otherwise, if someone tells me I'm wrong, it won't matter, I won't understand. That is the best I can do.

I heard Colin's door open, and his footsteps on the stairs. How long had we been sitting, how long since the phone call? I didn't know. Colin stopped in the living room entrance. We looked around. Bitsy smiled at Colin. He came around behind the couch, then sat next to Bitsy. He put his arm around her shoulders. He took her hand with his free hand. He put his head on her shoulder. She kissed his hair, then rested her cheek there. If the mute world denied us speech and thought, we would try something else.

The three of us went to the morgue on the day after the blizzard. We watched out the front windows for the snow plow, not at all sure we wanted it to come.

But it came, giving back a piece of the familiar terrain. There was the road, the trees, the lake. Colin and I shoveled the sidewalk.

Bitsy called a cab, and it took more than an hour to arrive. The driver described in detail his difficulties in getting to the house. From wherever you were there was only one way to get to where you were going. You had to seek out the cleared main roads. All the side streets were still dead-ended with snow. The driver was clearly enjoying himself. Bitsy told him we were going to the morgue. His animation ceased. We would have preferred that he continued his chatter. We would have liked the rest of the world to take U.T.'s death in stride, as we had not. It was nothing so unusual. I imagined:

"So, where can I take you?"

"County morgue, please."

"What, somebody die?"

"Yes, my husband, the father of my children. This is Colin, and Bryce, my youngest."

"Too bad. How'd it happen?"

"He threw himself from the Washington Avenue Bridge, sowed his vital spirit on the winds and died upon striking the river ice."

"The ice, huh?"

"Yes, it's the thickest in years."

"That's quite a fall."

"His momentum was considerable."

I almost laughed, I was so tired.

But we sat silent. We played with the buttons of our coats and watched cars sliding and spinning their wheels, and snow-plows plowing. The day was clear and sunny. The glare off the snow was almost unbearable. Southern air had sucked in after the storm, and the temperature was rising. The freeze would likely break today.

The driver let us out in front of a square 1960s brick building. He tried to refuse the tip, but Bitsy insisted. He asked if he should wait, meter off, and Bitsy said no.

A scruffy young man led us through antiseptic corridors to a large room with steel tables and a wall of deep drawers. He opened one drawer and U.T. came out. It was not, in fact, my father, only his mostly lifeless cells, but the illusion was powerful. That was not U.T., that stony pale face.

We looked. The young man stood by, jingling keys. I had an odd sense of recognition, but it was not simply seeing my father. I shivered suddenly and then I realized: it was the statue I was seeing, the shepherd with the lamb. As Bitsy had described it to me I had imagined U.T.'s face on the shepherd, U.T., a husk of mute bronze. I looked at Bitsy. I knew, I thought, she was thinking the same thing. She was fingering her nail-raw palms and wishing for blindness. By the laying on of hands, by the making of a world chosen and not imposed, she would return him to life. She would shape his face, trunk, and limbs; she would make every one of the hairs in his red beard, and draw in the crescent scar on his cheek, now swollen and purpled on the grayish skin. She would hold a cold thigh and cause it to warm and liven, warming and healing her own sore hands. Then she would lift her hands and suffer her blindness for the life it had bought. She would weep from the magic of making.

But that was not U.T., not that blanched chill face. U.T. came from the inside out. There was no more inside. Neither blindness nor magic hands would avail. Colin turned to the young man, who had begun to jingle his keys more loudly.

—It's him, Colin said. It is he.

Colin and I each took one of Bitsy's arms. We turned and left the long room with the deep drawers. The young man silenced his keys and shut the drawer of U.T.

❧

Various relatives, variously removed, came and went through the house in the days before the funeral. Mostly, I remember their leaving. A few of U.T.'s Vermont relatives passed through our door, mostly weeping; the prodigal son never came home. Who knows what's become of the fatted calf, grown and calved its own, by now.

Our prairie relations, the ones we only saw at weddings and funerals, stood in clutches muttering pieties. One cousin

I had never met—I heard he flew in from California with some kind of aunt or great-aunt I had never met—said to me,

—It's too bad the only time the family gets together is when somebody dies.

Somebody. Amen. You are young, my cousin, but you will die, you'll be that somebody someday. I thought I'd heard a song like that.

Bitsy's parents brought several baskets of fruit and cheeses and sausages.

After the funeral, I volunteered to clean out U.T.'s office. It would be easier for me than for Colin. The department secretary greeted me. She said she was very sorry about U.T. and, parenthetically, about our cat. I turned around to accept her condolences. There was an awkward moment as we faced each other at dueling distance. I nodded, mumbled thanks, and continued down the hall.

When I closed the door behind me in the small gray office, I felt safe. The office was in its usual vital disarray. As I looked more closely I saw the disfigured jade plant, and its flaccid squeezed leaves on the desk. The desk calendar was damp. In the ashtray there were three long ashes where three cigarettes had burned away untouched. I emptied the ashtray, swept the jade leaves into the wastebasket, and wadded the calendar in. I sat in the desk chair, where I had never sat before. Across from me was the poster and U.T.'s black-and-white image. *"The fancy cheats so well . . ."* I got up, tore down the poster, and started cleaning up. The secretary had left several cardboard boxes into which I placed the contents of the file cabinet. Most of the papers seemed expendable—scribbled lecture notes and exam questions, magazines and clippings—until I reached the top drawer. There I found U.T.'s journal and poems. I had seen all the poems, so I set them aside. I skimmed the thick journal, reading a passage here and there. I wasn't sure if I should have been reading it. On one page I saw a note in quotations. It was headed, "Augustine, *City of God.*" It read,

Mere existence is desirable in virtue of a kind of natural property [!]. So much so that even those who are wretched are for this very reason unwilling to die.

[U.T.'s note: For what reason? Because they are wretched? Do they know and love life more strongly in their wretchedness? And damn the natural property, the wretched continue in their wretchedness only in the hope that things will get better. If they knew as truth that wretchedness were their final destination, they would have no more of Augustine's "natural property." Existence is not desirable; it is imposed. Pass the ammunition! (But why do the wretched hope at all, when there is no reasonable ground for hope?)]

I stuck on the quotation and U.T.'s comment. One of the relatives who had arrived for the funeral, a pious Dakota aunt, had taken Bitsy's arm and announced to her,

—He's somewhere better now.

Yes, I thought, if you're better off dead. Who knows? I wondered if U.T. knew. It's a risk, either way, the whole thing is pretty chancy. Clearly, by U.T.'s testimony, you couldn't believe everything you read. Pious aunt, I thought, we'll never know.

I flipped through more pages, looking for some definitive statement, nothing so garish as a suicide note, but something. I remembered one of U.T.'s favorite lines, from Dylan Thomas: *I shall not murder / The mankind of her going with a grave truth . . .* Surely, he wouldn't murder his own. I stopped looking. I remembered more of the poems U.T. used to quote, and they began to make some kind of sense. Exactly what kind, I was not sure. I put the journal in the box with the poems and turned to the papers piled on the desk. One of the stacks contained essays from U.T.'s Romantic poetry class. In spite of the fact that the people who had written them were alive, I felt less guilty reading the papers than reading U.T.'s journal. I was always interested in what people had to say when they had sat down and thought about it, and I felt I had a fairly good grasp on the poetry through simple osmosis. In the first paper I read I found this lovely passage:

What is a bird? A feathered biped descended from lizards. Its feathers once were scales. What is its song? Waves sent out from vibrations of tiny cords, which sound to us as they do by virtue of our particular aural equipment. What is the Nightingale? A feathered biped of the genus *Daulias*, most commonly of the species *luscinia*. It sings most vividly of nights in the breeding season. It is a small European thrush.

After that the paper went all to hell. The writer was a biology major who went on about the feeding habits and digestive tract of the nightingale, and included a brief polemic on the vile fallacy of supposedly scientific but in fact heinously subjective Latin epithets such as *luscinia*, which is related, etymologically, to "luscious" and "lush," and which was utterly inappropriate in referring to a mere feathered biped descended from lizards, no matter how vividly it sang under hormonal influence. I skipped through the anatomy of thrushes and saw that U.T. had given the paper a "B." This surprised me, until I read a few more and found that he had given every one of them a "B." U.T.'s final comment on a mediocre generation. The fault reflected back on him: his generation had done this generating. But there was the old problem of assigning blame . . .

In defense of my generation, I fixed on a bold scheme. I would read all the papers, mask U.T.'s grades with correction fluid and regrade them according to worth. I started in, confidently, and after three or four papers I was in over my head. Like the labeling of nightingales, this task was hopelessly subjective. I continued reading, trying to formulate some scale of judgment. I was learning the value of expression. My generation did not yet know enough to protest. Neither did we feel strongly enough not to care that we didn't know, and realize that when we finally thought we knew it would be too late. Timidly, I put the bottle of correction fluid away.

The second stack of papers, it turned out, held poems by Caroline, the infamous, the legendary Caroline, rather pretty, brown-haired, suspected of desiring to be a concubine. I turned the pages over and leafed through them. I knew U.T. had not read them, because they were unmarked. U.T. was never without his red pen. Another product of the mediocre generation, he had laid them aside, assigning to them, perhaps, a mental "B." Or, he thought that reading the poems would embarrass him, and he always avoided embarrassment. Or, he was on his way to kill himself and simply didn't have time.

I looked at the poem on top of the pile. It was not embarrassing, at all. It was a poem that would have joyed and amazed U.T., all the more for its origins, but he had not read it. It was called "The Saint and the Stone," and it was headed with this note:

On Church Island in Lough Beg, Co. Derry, there is a stone in the churchyard with an oval depression. Legend holds that St. Patrick knelt there to pray, and his knee left the mark in the stone. Pilgrims come to bathe their afflictions in the rainwater that collects in the Saint's knee-mark.

I

On a bog island stone in Lough Beg
    Patrick genuflects.
The fog discovers him kneeling.

Now as then he brings knee to rock,
    Stony-kneed saint.
The fen surrounds him like prayer.

As legends go, this one is true;
    Saint Patrick kneeled;
His knees burned wounds in the stone.

The saint would rise early to encounter
    The frost-bitten hill
And praise his God from the stony ground.

One morning on that cold stone such heat
    As his faith produced
Marked this stone, this place, as holy.

II

What truck has a saint with a stone?
    The folk believe,
We folk believe, that the rain

Which gathers in Patrick's knee-hole
    Is blessed.
On the churchyard scrub we leave the rags

With which we salve our wounds with a dip
    Of holy water.
We shudder. What faith burns sockets in stone?

Cartilage cracks in the damp.
    A crowd gathers
On the firm ground; Patrick bans the serpent.

We look from the wood, 'cross the bog
    To the firm turf
Where saints walk. On Church Island

Saint Patrick kneeled, we know, a saint
    In the wilderness.
But for this, a bow to the stone had sufficed.

This was not the Caroline I knew through U.T. and Colin. I was saddened and angered that U.T. could have misjudged so badly, that he, of all people, could have missed this. At last, I was angry with U.T. I was angry, and I cried. Poor U.T., poor Caroline, poor Colin, so recently so happy, so stupid and blind, all of them. I hated our illusions. It made me sick that we needed them, so I cried.

There was a light knock on the door, and the secretary came in. She saw that I was crying and started to back out, but I motioned her in. She came to the desk with a cup of coffee for me. She set the coffee on the desk. She looked at me. She asked if she could help. I said no. She stood for a moment, patting the edge of the desk as she would pat my head or shoulder. She wanted me to yield and confess, I thought, so she could comfort me. They all wanted that, something to do, some weapon against death and grief; it was more disturbing to be on the edge of it. I thanked her for the coffee and she left.

I turned and looked out the window, U.T.'s last window, and saw the Washington Avenue Bridge in the sun. The bridge was busy with students, East Bank, West Bank, fifteen minutes passing time. I held Caroline's poem on my lap. I looked at the poem, I looked out the window. I thought: *Father, why didn't you read this? These few minutes might have saved your faith, saved your life, saved the world. There is hope:* I closed my eyes: *There is hope.*

I sat with my eyes closed, holding Caroline's poem. When I felt a little better I went back to clearing off the desk. At the edge of the desk there was a single sheet of paper, dampened by jade leaf water. I turned it over. It was a poem U.T. had been working on. The first three lines of the first stanza were crossed out, something about adjectives sprung and flung. The second stanza was complete. The writing was blurred by the wet, but I was able to make it out. It read:

> Silence presses like the weight
> Of deep water. The moments
> Come and go. The waters, once so rich
> With sense, are empty now
> Of meaning, and the weight of the world
> As object betrays our ancient hopes.

Of the third stanza there were two lines:

> I wake under water from a dream
> Of the world strangely lighted.

It was good, I thought, but I didn't know. I couldn't be objective. I wondered if U.T. had awakened under water, and what kind of weight that was. I tried to blot the page dry, but succeeded only in blurring the words further.

Someone slipped something under the door. I went over and picked it up. It was the University newspaper. A banner headline across the top of the front page read: "Ulysses Turner Fraser: 'The life of the English department . . .'" I glanced over the copy: a colorful reputation, Eastern flair, cosmopolitan outlook, a credit to his profession, a superb stylist. Something to remember him by. *His momentum was considerable, a Darkness borne downward.*

❧

We received visits from friends and relatives for several days after the funeral. We dressed in nice clothes, and we were polite and sad. The house filled with flowers and food.

Colin, Bitsy, and I sat in the living room after the departure of a wave of guests. The jade plant from U.T.'s office sat near the fireplace. The branches on one side were bare of leaves. We were exhausted from having to dress in nice clothes and be sad and polite.

We heard a sound, like a cricket. There was a flutter of translucent wings on the jade plant. A green insect sat there, singing. I thought it was a katydid, but Bitsy said it was a snowy tree cricket. It was smaller than a katydid, and a brighter shade of green. It sang on. We smiled.

On the third night, as the snow and wind continued, I thought, there ought to be something more, an up-date, further information. But after the phone call there was only silence and our loneliness. U.T. was out there, somewhere, dead, and we were here. We sat. I got up and laid a fire in the fireplace. The good dry wood caught quickly. We watched the fire. What would life be like without U.T.? What was life like, at all? Like nothing you've ever seen, I thought. And what do we know of it? I thought, we don't.

Colin said,

—I saw someone on the bridge as the bus pulled away. I don't know, it must have been. I was on my way to see him.

Then the might-haves and should-haves and could-haves closed in on us, the terror of cause and possibility. Bitsy got up and went to the kitchen. When she returned she had a tray with a bottle of port and three glasses, and a plate with crackers and a few slices of cheese. She set the tray down and poured the port and gave us each a glass. I looked through the glass at the light, the rich red filled with light. I looked at the white crackers on the plate. I sipped my port and took a small bite of a cracker. I remembered the mock confirmation ceremony and U.T.'s fury. I understood. Bitsy had been right, it was not funny, it was not a jest. U.T. knew that, too. I knew why Bitsy had cried. It was not from shame or the profaning of the holy. It had not been a flip or trivial act, and neither was this, this wine, these white crackers.

I did not quite understand. Nor, I thought, had my father understood.

I looked at Bitsy and Colin. We sipped our port and nibbled crackers. We all knew what this was, but that didn't matter. I thought of the Joyce story, "The Sisters." Life followed fiction. But the instant I thought it, it was fiction following fiction. That was the way the world went, it was becoming clear, fiction following fiction by no dint of cause, by blithe associations. It was appropriate. Acts of communion had always been U.T.'s favorite bits of symbolism. He thought Hemingway got it just right with the trout and wineskins.

We raised our glasses in a silent toast. We drank, we ate dry white crackers.

On the third night Colin dreamed again the dream of the Narrator. The shopkeeper showed him the display of the dead, so many, yes, he remembered, there had been many. The Narrator appeared and haunted Colin's flight through the halls of the English department that was also our house. The Narrator died and was reborn on the hand of someone taken for a friend. In the dream Colin thought: the friend is my father, the friend must be my father. But it was not. The friend was faceless, as before, some generic friend and betrayer. Marcos got mixed up in the dream—the Narrator was a crag-faced shaman for a while. The Narrator had many faces. He had the face of the true Ramon, the savior dead in the jungle; he had the face of all the horrible dead.

It was morning and bright when Colin awoke. He heard water dripping from the eaves. Marcos was dead. No, Marcos lived. Which was it? Where was the truth? Colin did not know, just yet.

I dreamed the Emperors of China. I was the pheasant's shadow, running helter-skelter over a rough terrain, running on heedless.

Colin took U.T.'s box of souvenirs from the bedroom closet. He spread them on his desk and looked at them, held them. These were things our father had touched, in which he had placed some meaning—a leaf, a stone, postcards, bric-a-brac, junk. Colin scanned them as if reading a sacred text. The arrangement of objects was like an experimental novel: all of these things are connected; you must discover how they fit; you must become U.T. Fraser to do it. There are several ways to approach this task, any number of which might kill you.

Colin packed away the souvenirs. He would make his own way. He began the fictional biography of Ulysses Turner Fraser.

Ulysses Turner Fraser was born in the labyrinthine hills of Vermont, the son of simple hills folk. Very early he knew the meanings of words, the power of a phrase. The landscape was alive to him. He was named not in vain for the fabulous voyager. He felt in his heart the pull of the mythical man.

As he grew, the world came to oppress him. He sought the mystery behind the manifest, and he worked at knowing mystery. He labored like an ox under his consciousness. Something was wrong, something was lost; he sought to return it.

It did not go. Colin started again:

—Birthdays: the ineluctable mementos of mortality, my father said first thing in the morning.

It was January. It was cold, the fifty-fifth straight day below freezing.

He stalled. What more could you say? He put it aside. He needed more distance. He thought about the man on the bridge. Perhaps that was where to start. A glimpse from the back of the bus. Who is that man on the bridge? Why is he there, and what does he intend? Start with the bridge on an ordinary day. The day falls into place. It is horror and beauty at once. Who would have thought?

We sipped our port as the fire died down. We nibbled at crackers and cheese. The world slowly softened around us. Things gently refused to speak. The world rebuked the triumph of logic. I thought of the drifts outside the kitchen window, and the image was pleasing. That was the way the world went, and it was best to accord with it; it was essential to pay attention.

Later, we would not know these hours, the spread of the long third night. We would remember them, but we would never believe in them. We would feel the rough nick of buried memory, and this night would be the referent, but we would not know it, or we would deny it. A line of poetry or some flickering vision would set it off, a door would open and close; we would shield our eyes, or pinch them shut, shout at the tops of our lungs, fierce denunciations. We could believe anything we chose to believe; we could make anything as true as it could be.

The snow sifted down through the dark hours of the long third night. The drifts shifted, rose and fell, the wind rattled and the furnace burned. We sighed and settled. The burning logs fell and crumbled. We sipped port and ate dry crackers, no trivial act. We touched and wondered.